D1601472

The Spirit of
the Constitution

A DECADE OF STUDY OF THE CONSTITUTION

How Democratic Is the Constitution?
Robert A. Goldwin and William A. Schambra, editors

How Capitalistic Is the Constitution?
Robert A. Goldwin and William A. Schambra, editors

How Does the Constitution Secure Rights?
Robert A. Goldwin and William A. Schambra, editors

Separation of Powers: Does It Still Work?
Robert A. Goldwin and Art Kaufman, editors

How Federal Is the Constitution?
Robert A. Goldwin and William A. Schambra, editors

How Does the Constitution Protect Religious Freedom?
Robert A. Goldwin and Art Kaufman, editors

Slavery and Its Consequences:
The Constitution, Equality, and Race
Robert A. Goldwin and Art Kaufman, editors

The Constitution, the Courts, and the Quest for Justice
Robert A. Goldwin and William A. Schambra, editors

Foreign Policy and the Constitution
Robert A. Goldwin and Robert A. Licht, editors

The Spirit of the Constitution: Five Conversations
Robert A. Goldwin and Robert A. Licht, editors

The Spirit of the Constitution

Five Conversations

Robert A. Goldwin
and Robert A. Licht,
editors

The AEI Press

Publisher for the American Enterprise Institute
WASHINGTON, D.C.

1990

This book is the tenth, and final, in a series in AEI's project "A Decade of Study of the Constitution," funded in part by grants from the National Endowment for the Humanities. A full list of titles appears on the series page.

Distributed by arrangement with

University Press of America, Inc.
4720 Boston Way   3 Henrietta Street
Lanham, Md. 20706   London WC2E 8LU England

Library of Congress Cataloging-in-Publication Data

The spirit of the Constitution: five conversations / Robert A.
Goldwin and Robert A. Licht, editors.
    p.   cm.
    ISBN 0-8447-3719-4 (alk. paper). — ISBN 0-8447-3720-8 (alk. paper pbk.)
    1. United States—Constitutional law—Interpretation and construction.   I. Goldwin, Robert A., 1922–   .   II. Licht, Robert A.   III. American Enterprise Institute for Public Policy Research.
KF4550.F58   1990
342.73'029—dc20
[347.30229]   89-18585
                                                              CIP

1   3   5   7   9   10   8   6   4   2

AEI Studies 506

The AEI Press
Publisher for the American Enterprise Institute
1150 Seventeenth Street, N.W., Washington, D.C. 20036

Printed in the United States of America

Contents

Foreword

These five conversations on the spirit of the Constitution compose the tenth and final volume of the American Enterprise Institute's series, A Decade of Study of the Constitution, celebrating our Constitution's bicentennial.

The text of the Constitution is surprisingly lacking in spirit. Most of the state constitutions written before the federal Constitution were quite different—they were explicit about the essential character of their institutions, the ultimate aims they were to serve, and the character their citizens were to have. The Massachusetts Constitution of 1780, for example, contained thirty lengthy articles following the preamble, describing in great detail the origins and purpose of society and government, the natural and civil rights citizens were to enjoy and the duties they were expected to perform, the moral qualities offices and officeholders were to exhibit, and the character of elections and other political institutions.

The Constitution of the United States contains little of this; following the brief Preamble, it is strictly business. On its surface it is little more than a matter-of-fact account of the structure and powers of the new government. Indeed many insist that this is all the Constitution was ever meant to be and that it is foolish, or even dangerous, to try to read more into it.

Still, most of us—and not only loose constructionists—believe that there is more to the Constitution than is explicitly described in its text. We commonly speak of the Constitution's principles—separation of powers, federalism, separation of church and state, checks and balances, and so forth—although these terms do not appear in the text. We often describe various political purposes the constitutional arrangements are supposed to serve—such as liberty, equality, democracy, and, recently, privacy—even though we cannot point to a provision mandating them. And everyday American political dialogue is conducted as if rooted in the Constitution even when the text itself is silent.

That we speak and act as if there is an unspoken spirit of the Constitution is certainly not proof of its existence. But it does indicate that the spirit is something worth looking into, for whether there is such a spirit has deep significance for the great national enterprise the

American people have been engaged in for the last two hundred years. The search for that spirit in this volume proves, if proof be needed, that we are still inspirited by the Constitution and that, in our diversity, this unites us.

The Constitution project of the American Enterprise Institute has contributed a unique intellectual perspective to the public policy dialogue because it has taken as its theme the purposes and ideas embodied in our fundamental charter. The founding father and animating spirit of the Constitution project has been Robert A. Goldwin, who in addition to his own written contributions has done a magnificent job of intellectual orchestration here as in many other scholarly endeavors. In the bicentennial series alone, he and his associates have produced nine other volumes of essays on the great themes of the Constitution: democracy, in *How Democratic Is the Constitution?*; capitalism, in *How Capitalistic Is the Constitution?*; federalism, in *How Federal Is the Constitution?*; individual rights, in *How Does the Constitution Secure Rights?*; religion, in *How Does the Constitution Protect Religious Freedom?*; the structure of government, in *Separation of Powers: Does It Still Work?*; race, in *Slavery and Its Consequences: The Constitution, Equality, and Race*; justice, in *The Constitution, the Courts, and the Quest for Justice*; and foreign relations, in *Foreign Policy and the Constitution*. The present and final volume appropriately shows that the dialogue is a continuing one.

Christopher C. DeMuth
President
American Enterprise Institute

Preface

Let the end be legitimate, let it be within the scope of the Constitution, and all means which are appropriate, which are plainly adapted to that end, which are not prohibited, but consistent with the letter and spirit of the constitution [*emphasis added*], *are constitutional.*
                                    —John Marshall, *McCulloch v. Maryland*

Chief Justice Marshall, writing in 1819, was comfortable with the notion that there is a "spirit of the constitution" in a way that perhaps many today are not. Since the time of Marshall a great body of jurisprudence has grown up around the Constitution, much of it technical and inaccessible to nonlawyers, with the result that today it is commonplace to mean constitutional law when we speak of the Constitution. This lends discussions of constitutional topics a legalistic, literalistic character that rarely admits of matters so free and wide-ranging as the word "spirit" would imply. And yet it is neither metaphysical nor poetic to insist that we may well fail to see the Constitution for what it is if we do not search for its spirit.

Marshall himself is our authority in this, for his decisions took into account what he called "the great objects" of the Constitution, by which he meant the character of, and the conditions for bringing into existence, the popular self-government that the framers hoped to establish. These great objects have a claim to being thought of as the spirit of the Constitution. They are the *unspoken* principles of the charter. "Separation of powers," "federalism," and "separation of church and state," for example, are words and phrases not mentioned in the text of the Constitution, but most people do not question that each of them is an integral part of the Constitution. It is such unspoken principles that we refer to when we speak of the spirit of the Constitution.

A Decade of Study of the Constitution, the American Enterprise Institute's contribution to the bicentennial of the Constitution (of which this volume is the tenth and last in the series), took as its stated goal an inquiry into the original, unamended Constitution that the framers wrote in 1787. The premise of the inquiry is that the Constitution is the source of our national life, the way we have chosen to constitute ourselves as a people. Although most study of constitutional questions today is the study of constitutional law, the study of decisions of the Supreme Court as distinguished from the study of the Constitution itself, we chose to consider the Constitution not just as a legal document but as the fundamental political, social, and economic framework of American government and society.

Our quest then is in accord with Marshall's reflections on the great objects of the framers' Constitution. Our object is to reach back into the spirit of the framers' deliberations at the time of the Constitutional Convention. It is fitting therefore that our series and our ten-year effort conclude with conversations, deliberations, on the great objects, the spirit of the Constitution.

If we think about what the great objects of the Constitution might be, surely the list would include some of the following: that we preserve the federal structure of the government, to encourage a large measure of self-rule in all parts of the country; that we strive to be a prosperous people, free to pursue a livelihood according to our individual choices; that we steadily enhance the democratic character of the nation, that is, that all of our political, economic, and social activities be pursued in accordance with democratic principles and practice, and that this be done without violating our commitment to liberty and equality; and, finally, that we conduct ourselves in a manner befitting the religious traditions so powerful among us from our earliest beginnings as Americans. It is these five great objects (and there surely are others) that inspirit the Constitution and that our panels discuss in their search for the spirit of the Constitution.

In these conversations we are searching for some way to capture and describe the unspoken principles, the undefined and elusive spirit. We raise the question whether it is to be found in the federal character, commerce, democracy, liberty and equality, religion, or some combination of them. Five panels of distinguished scholars, jurists, and journalists were assembled to address each of the above topics in turn. Each panel was asked the same question: In what ways and to what extent could each of these topics be considered as a part of the spirit of the Constitution? This volume is a record of their insightful and spirited conversations.

ROBERT A. GOLDWIN
ROBERT A. LICHT

The Editors and the Participants

ROBERT A. GOLDWIN is resident scholar and director of constitutional studies at the American Enterprise Institute. He served in the White House as special consultant to the president and concurrently as adviser to the secretary of defense. Mr. Goldwin has taught at the University of Chicago and Kenyon College and was dean of St. John's College in Annapolis. He is the editor of more than a score of books on American politics, coeditor of the AEI series of volumes on the Constitution, and author of *Why Blacks, Women, and Jews Are Not Mentioned in the Constitution, and Other Unorthodox Views* (1990).

ROBERT A. LICHT is a visiting scholar and associate director of the Constitution project at the American Enterprise Institute. Mr. Licht has taught at Bucknell University and St. John's College, Annapolis, and has been a visiting scholar at the Kennedy Center for Ethics at Georgetown University and a National Endowment for the Humanities fellow at AEI. He has written articles about the American founding and the nature of American political institutions. Mr. Licht is coeditor of *Foreign Policy and the Constitution*.

WILLIAM B. ALLEN is professor of government at Harvey Mudd College, former chairman of the U.S. Commission on Civil Rights, and program director of the Liberty Fund Bicentennial Project. His recent publications include *A Washington Reader* (forthcoming), *The Essential Antifederalist, The Works of Fisher Ames*, and "Slavery in American Politics."

EDWARD C. BANFIELD is the George D. Markham Professor of Government Emeritus at Harvard University. He has written extensively on American politics, especially the problems of American cities and political party reform. His books include *City Politics* (with James Q. Wilson), *The Moral Basis of a Backward Society* (with Laura Banfield), *The Unheavenly City*, and *The Democratic Muse*.

BENJAMIN R. BARBER is professor of political science at Rutgers University and the author of many books, including *Strong Democracy* and *The Conquest of Politics* (forthcoming). He contributes regularly to

Harper's and *New Republic* and is working on a ten-part television series entitled "The Struggle for Democracy."

HERMAN BELZ is professor of history at the University of Maryland. He is the author of several works on civil rights history, law, and public policy, including *A New Birth of Freedom: The Republican Party and Freedmen's Rights, 1861–1866, Emancipation and Equal Rights: Politics and Constitutionalism in the Civil War Era*, and *Affirmative Action from Kennedy to Reagan: Redefining American Equality.* Mr. Belz is coauthor of *The American Constitution: Its Origins and Development.*

WALTER BERNS is the John M. Olin University Professor at Georgetown University and adjunct scholar at the American Enterprise Institute. He has written many books and articles on constitutional issues, including *The First Amendment and the Future of American Democracy, For Capital Punishment, In Defense of Liberal Democracy,* and most recently *Taking the Constitution Seriously.* Mr. Berns was a member of the National Council on the Humanities and served on the U.S. delegation to the United Nations Commission on Human Rights.

EVA T. H. BRANN is a tutor at St. John's College, Annapolis. She has been the Arnold Distinguished Visiting Professor at Whitman College, Honors Professor at the University of Delaware, and a National Endowment for the Humanities fellow. Ms. Brann is the author of *Paradoxes of Education in a Republic* and essays on such diverse topics as the Gettysburg Address, the novels of Jane Austen and Thomas Mann, and music in Plato's *Republic.*

AMY BRIDGES is visiting professor of political science at Stanford University and in 1990 will join the faculty of the University of California at San Diego. Her first book, *A City in the Republic,* is about the origins of machine politics. She is researching the urban Southwest and municipal reform.

JAMES CEASER is professor of government and foreign affairs at the University of Virginia. He is the author of *Presidential Selection: Theory and Development,* which won the Phi Beta Kappa prize at the University of Virginia in 1979; *Proportional Representation in Presidential Nomination Politics;* and *Reforming the Reforms.*

JOSEPH CROPSEY is the Distinguished Service Professor in Political Science at the University of Chicago, where he has taught political philosophy for the past thirty years. He is the author or editor of

books and articles on political philosophy, including *Polity and Economy: An Interpretation of Adam Smith*, *History of Political Philosophy*
(coeditor with Leo Strauss and contributing author), and *Political Philosophy and the Issues of Politics*.

DAVID EPSTEIN is deputy director of net assessment, Office of the
Secretary of Defense, and has been a professor of political science at
the New School for Social Research. He is the author of *The Political
Theory of the Federalist* and other articles on American political
thought.

CHARLES H. FAIRBANKS, JR., is research professor of international
relations at the Johns Hopkins School of Advanced International Studies and directs the Foreign Policy Institute's Program in Soviet and
American National Security Policymaking. He has served as deputy
assistant secretary of state for human rights and has taught at the
University of Toronto and Yale University.

HARVEY FLAUMENHAFT is a tutor at St. John's College, Annapolis. He
has taught at the University of Chicago, Roosevelt University, and
Wheaton College (Massachusetts) and is the author of articles on the
thought of Alexander Hamilton and the presidency of George Washington. Mr. Flaumenhaft is working on a series of guidebooks for the
humanistic study of classics texts in science.

MORTON J. FRISCH is professor of political science at Northern Illinois
University. He has written extensively on American political thought
and modern political theory, including his book *Franklin D. Roosevelt:
The Contribution of the New Deal to American Political Thought and Prac-
tice*. He is also editor of *Selected Writings and Speeches of Alexander
Hamilton* and of *American Political Thought: The Philosophic Dimensions of
American Statesmanship*.

A. E. DICK HOWARD is the White Burkett Miller Professor of Law and
Public Affairs at the University of Virginia Law School. An authority
on constitutional law, Mr. Howard directed the revision of Virginia's
Constitution from 1968 to 1970. His books and articles include *The
Road from Runnymede: Magna Carta and Constitutionalism in America* and
Commentaries on the Constitution of Virginia.

CHARLES KRAUTHAMMER is senior editor at the *New Republic* and a
syndicated columnist with the *Washington Post*. He was a contributing
essayist at *Time*, speechwriter for Vice President Walter Mondale,

director of the Division of Research for the Alcohol, Drug Abuse, and Mental Health Administration at the Department of Health and Human Services, and chief resident of the Psychiatric Consultation Service, Massachusetts General Hospital.

IRVING KRISTOL is the John M. Olin Professor of Social Thought at the New York University Graduate School of Business Administration, coeditor of the *Public Interest*, publisher of the *National Interest*, and senior fellow at the American Enterprise Institute. He writes a monthly article for the *Wall Street Journal* and is the author of *On the Democratic Idea in America*, *Two Cheers for Capitalism*, and *Reflections of a Neoconservative*.

WILLIAM KRISTOL is assistant to the vice president for domestic policy. Before this appointment, he served as chief of staff and counselor to the secretary of education while on leave from teaching public policy at the John F. Kennedy School of Government, Harvard University. Mr. Kristol is the author of essays and articles on American political thought and the American judiciary appearing in *Social Philosophy and Policy*, *Chicago Law Review*, *Harvard Journal of Law and Public Policy*, and *Public Interest*.

TERENCE MARSHALL is professor of judicial and political sciences at the University of Paris X-Nanterre. He taught political science at the University of Pennsylvania, North Carolina State University, and the University of Paris I-Sorbonne-Pantheon. Mr. Marshall has written articles on political philosophy, constitutional theory, and American politics for such journals as *Revue Francaise de Science Politique*, *Revue de Synthese*, *Revue de Metaphysique et de Morale*, and *Political Theory* and is working on a two-volume study of the theory and practice of American constitutional government.

ABNER MIKVA is a judge on the U.S. Court of Appeals for the District of Columbia Circuit. He has been a member of the Illinois House of Representatives and a member of Congress from Illinois. In Congress Mr. Mivka served on the Judiciary and the Ways and Means Committees and was chairman of the Democratic Study Group.

ROBERT NOVAK writes a syndicated column, "Inside Report," with Rowland Evans and is a regular panelist on the television news commentary program "The McLaughlin Group." He is the author of *The Agony of the GOP* and is coauthor of *Lyndon B. Johnson: The Exercise of Power, Nixon in the White House: The Frustration of Power,* and *The Reagan Revolution.*

MARC F. PLATTNER is director of program development at the National Endowment for Democracy and editor of the *Journal of Democracy.* He was adviser on economic and social affairs at the U.S. Mission to the United Nations, managing editor of the *Public Interest,* and director of issues research for the Moynihan for Senate Campaign in 1976. Mr. Plattner is the author of *Rousseau's State of Nature* and editor of *Human Rights in Our Time*

JACK N. RAKOVE is professor of history and director of the American studies program at Stanford University. He is the author of *The Beginnings of National Politics: An Interpretive History of the Continental Congress* and articles on constitutional history and politics, including "Mr. Meese, Meet Mr. Madison" (*Atlantic Monthly,* December 1986).

LAURENCE H. SILBERMAN is a judge on the U.S. Court of Appeals for the District of Columbia Circuit. He has served as under secretary of labor, deputy attorney general, and ambassador to Yugoslavia. Mr. Silberman is adjunct professor of law at the Georgetown University Law Center.

ROGER STARR is a member of the editorial board of the *New York Times.* He was administrator and commissioner of the Housing and Development Administration for New York City and is the author of *Urban Choices, Housing and the Money Market, America's Housing Challenge,* and most recently *The Rise and Fall of New York City.*

PATRICIA M. WALD is a judge on the U.S. Court of Appeals for the District of Columbia Circuit. She was assistant attorney general for legislative affairs and an attorney for the Center for Law and Social Policy, the Neighborhood Legal Services Program, and the Office of Criminal Justice, Department of Justice. Ms. Wald has written on criminal justice, juvenile law, mental disability law, poverty law, and the judicial process.

J. CLIFFORD WALLACE is a judge on the U.S. Court of Appeals for the Ninth Circuit. He was a judge on the U.S. District Court for the Southern District of California. Mr. Wallace has been a visiting or adjunct professor at three law schools. The author of articles on constitutional interpretation and administrative problems of the judiciary, he wrote *Judicial Administration in a System of Independents: A Tribe with Only Chiefs.*

JEAN YARBROUGH is professor of government and legal studies at Bowdoin College. She has written on federalism, representation, commerce, property, character, and republicanism in the American founding. Ms. Yarbrough, a bicentennial fellow of the National Endowment for the Humanities, is working on a study of the moral foundations of the American republic.

EDWIN M. YODER, JR., is a syndicated columnist with the *Washington Post* Writers' Group. He has been the editorial page editor of the *Washington Star,* the *Charlotte News,* and the *Greensboro Daily News* and professor of history at the University of North Carolina. Mr. Yoder received the Pulitzer Prize in 1979 for editorial writing. His articles have appeared in *Harper's, New Republic,* and *National Review.*

1
Federal Union

ROBERT GOLDWIN: In this discussion of federal union as an essential part of the spirit of the Constitution, we focus on the structure and processes established by the Constitution: First, there are states with a large measure of self-rule and independence; second, they are subordinated as elements in a union. As the Preamble states, "to establish a more perfect union" was a major reason for writing the new Constitution, well summed up in the motto, *e pluribus unum*, one out of many. At the time of the founding, "federal" and "union" were considered by some to be contradictory and considered by most to be in some sort of tension—federal pulling in one direction and union pulling in the other.

The federal aspect shows itself in many parts of the Constitution: for example, the electoral college for electing the president is a federal institution. The Senate is also federal in its system of representation, with two senators from each state, regardless of size, the states being, in that sense, equal. The constitutional provision that the advice and consent of the Senate is required for treaties and appointments is federal. And so are many other features of the Constitution.

We probably also ought to give time and thought to the structural aspects of the union, especially the complexities of the separation of powers. And so I put the question to the panel: To what extent and in what ways can it be said that the complex machinery of federal union is the spirit of the Constitution?

JAMES CEASER: Recently I looked through *The Federalist* to find a passage that relates closely to the question of this session, and I found a brief passage in *Federalist* No. 9 in which Alexander Hamilton lists many of the structural features that Mr. Goldwin mentioned, such as separation of powers and representation. Hamilton wrote as follows: "They are means, powerful means by which the excellencies of republican government may be retained, and its imperfections lessened or avoided."

That is a good starting point because under the first conception we have of "spirit," we normally think of the ends of the Constitution.

But the structural features are not ends. They are, as Hamilton says, means. That is, they are good and worthwhile only insofar as they promote certain ends. One cannot love separation of powers in the same way that one loves liberty or self-government. These structural features are means to certain ends, such as liberty, domestic tranquility, and peace.

The only exception to this—that the structural features are means and thus not the spirit of the Constitution—might be federal union itself because there is a sense today in which we think of "union" as being almost an end in itself. After all, we are patriotic about America. Commercials speak of the "heartbeat of America"; they do not speak of the heartbeat of Rhode Island. So there may be a sense in which the union itself is an end, and yet it becomes an end, in and of itself, only once it realizes certain of these broader ends.

There is, however, another sense in which we use the word "spirit," and that sometimes refers to what animates something. In this sense one can say that the structure is the spirit because the structure does animate the Constitution.

What we find primarily in the Constitution itself is an elaboration of powers. We can raise the question, Is the structure of the Constitution self-executing or self-maintaining? That is, will the Constitution keep going, as it was originally intended, merely by people being elected to the various offices that are described and performing in those offices? Does the structure maintain itself over time?

This question might serve as a point of discussion. There are powerful forces in the Constitution toward its self-maintenance. But in this same passage from Hamilton, he says that all of these structures are based on a certain understanding of political science. Perhaps we have to recover the political science that is at the root of these structures because without this political science it may well be that these structures are not self-maintaining.

JEAN YARBROUGH: Professor Ceaser's question was, Does the structure maintain itself over time? The state constitutions originally sought to perform a distinct and separate purpose, that of somehow forming the moral character of their citizens in a way that is no longer allowed to the state governments.

If in fact the state governments are no longer seen as complementary to the purposes of the federal government with respect to the character of the people, what has become of their function? Does the federal system in fact maintain itself? Is it capable of maintaining itself if it is no longer permitted to pursue the purposes that were originally assigned to it?

Mr. GOLDWIN: What changes have taken these functions away from the states?

Ms. YARBROUGH: The old state constitution of Massachusetts, for example, talks about the moral character of citizens and invites citizens to take into account the moral character of the representatives whom they are going to elect. The constitutions of Massachusetts, Vermont, New Hampshire, and Virginia all speak of the virtues that citizens are supposed to have if they are in fact to be capable of self-government. They go on to talk about how religion, morality, and piety, rightly grounded on evangelical principles, are the necessary mainstays of republican government.

All of these provisions, particularly the religion clauses, have certainly died away. The Supreme Court no longer permits the states to maintain a policy separate from that of the national government. If the national government is not allowed to become involved in religious questions, neither now are the state governments. Originally only the federal government was not permitted to involve itself in these questions; the state constitutions certainly did. They were expected to play a different role regarding religion, education, and moral character. This purpose no longer applies because the states are held to be microcosms of the federal government. Whatever is permitted the federal government is permitted to state governments, and whatever is not permitted the federal government is no longer permitted to the states.

There was a complementary relationship initially between the state constitutions and the federal Constitution. Now there is an identical relationship, and many of those original state purposes have simply disappeared.

DAVID EPSTEIN: Then, by implication, states become redundant, or unnecessary. The question is, How did this come about, if this is a correct characterization? And this relates to Mr. Ceaser's question of whether the institutions do maintain themselves. One aspect of the institutions is that they permit themselves to be changed through the process of amendment. The Fourteenth Amendment, which specifically ruled out certain state policies, marks a big change.

The amendment providing for direct election of senators is another big change because we no longer have representation of the state legislatures themselves in Congress to protect their authority. That representation in Congress was regarded as an important protection for the independent sphere of state activity. Senators might have been more receptive to Judge Bork's position defending state self-government against the claims of rights imposed by the federal judiciary had those senators been elected by the state legislatures that exercise that self-government.

In some respects the changes have been made deliberately. But the people who made those changes probably did not think through all of the implications and did not foresee exactly how they would affect the system as a whole.

One other consideration is that even from the founding this tendency to change the role of the states would meet with sympathy from certain of the founders. Madison and Hamilton, for example, looked forward to the day when the states would decline in importance. Madison opposed their efforts to shape the moral character of citizens by establishment of religion. He regarded the exercise of such powers as factious repression by narrow-minded people.

Madison did not quite get his way on this. One of the problems is that the federal union, as originally devised, was a compromise. There was an unclarity in the beginning about whether "a more perfect union" is one that more perfectly preserves the separateness of the parts or more perfectly unites the parts, and therefore tends to obliterate them. That is the tension between "federal" and "union."

MR. GOLDWIN: But will you clarify what you mean when you say that Madison did not get his way. What was Madison's hope or expectation on this subject?

MR. EPSTEIN: He did not get his proposal that the Congress should be allowed to veto state laws.

MR. GOLDWIN: The Constitution of the United States did not deal with matters regarding the morality and character of the citizenry because the state constitutions did. Madison's expectation or hope was that the states' power to do these things would diminish. Thus, in the end, Madison's way would give us the situation we now have; that is, no American constitution, state or national, tries to exert influence over the morality or character of the citizenry.

MR. EPSTEIN: You stated Madison's intention somewhat more strongly than I would. Madison would look with favor upon states taking an interest in the character of citizens by education, but he would consider establishment of religion, for example, as a case where a state's interest in citizens' character had an oppressive nature.

MR. GOLDWIN: Schools are all right, but not prayer?

MR. EPSTEIN: Yes.

WILLIAM KRISTOL: Do we need someone to defend school prayer? I am happy to do it. I agree with what has been said so far in one respect. It seems that the tendency was probably inevitable toward nationalizing, or toward eroding, the role of the states in shaping a way of life for citizens. And that nationalizing is in accord with the spirit of the Constitution in the sense that Articles IV and VI of the Constitution are really the decisive articles for they clearly establish the supremacy of the federal Constitution over the states.

At the founding, however, there was no expectation that the states would be active or forceful in shaping the character of citizens. Room was left for other associations—ranging from churches to voluntary associations to educational institutions—to shape the character of citizens. The erosion of the states' role has gone on longer than we tend to think and was in a sense more inevitable than we tend to say now. It cannot be put back. In this respect, Humpty Dumpty cannot be put back together again. No one, really, is interested any more in defending, or in arguing for, as a matter of public policy, restoring to the states the ability to shape the way of life of citizens.

That has been made impossible partly by modern commerce, technology, communications, and transportation, all of which are also more or less in the spirit of the Constitution. Presumably the founders would have been happy with the mobility and the instant communications. Perhaps they would not be happy with every aspect, but they would be more or less in accord with developments in that direction.

People move so much. They watch national television. People live, for example, in Maryland or Virginia suburbs of Washington, D.C., but do not really think of themselves as Marylanders or Virginians. There is inevitably an erosion of the notion that the state is a crucial entity standing for a moral vision or a certain way of life. This happened partly as a result of commerce, technology, and the like and partly as a result of constitutional amendments and Supreme Court interpretations of those amendments. Those things were not inevitable by any means and may not all have been desirable, but they cannot be rolled back in any major respect.

That does not mean that the states are now unimportant in all respects. From the point of view of public policy, the states are important, though in a more limited way, as Justice Brandeis, I think, said, as laboratories of experimentation in different policy areas. There is the field of education, for example. It is important that we have fifty different state systems. If something is introduced in one system and seems to work, we can then argue that it should be introduced in the others.

It very much affects the character of contemporary American politics, and public policy, that we have states with governors and state legislators who are directly elected by the people and are not subdivisions of the federal government. In this respect, America is different from England, France, and many other nations because our states really have independent policy-making authority and independent political bases. That is important in understanding public policy in many areas.

On the whole this is good for public policy. It leads to a kind of market phenomenon. In state tax policy, for example, states cannot pursue excessively irresponsible policies because businesses would leave and go to other states. This holds true somewhat in other areas like education. There is a certain healthy competition among states in areas of public policy, but that is different from states seeking to shape the character of the citizenry. That power cannot be restored.

Some of today's interesting public policy proposals indirectly address this issue of the character of the citizenry, and also involve strengthening state governments. There are proposals for selling public housing to the tenants. That is an example of privatization that would presumably encourage people to take more responsibility for their own lives. Workfare and ideas like that combat dependency. In many of those areas, the states are the relevant instrument of government, but in others, localities could be. There are strong arguments that the states should take a more active role in education, but there are also strong, and sometimes complementary, arguments that we should deregulate down to the school-building level, or even to the individual parent level, and encourage greater parental choice among schools.

One can think about public policy reforms in relation to a host of mechanisms and institutions, of which the states are one. But all of that is quite different from the notion of the states as fundamental in shaping the life of citizens.

MR. GOLDWIN: Whenever we experience a national presidential election, do we not see evidence of the persistence of the importance of states, and their tremendous diversity, as candidates try to garner votes in one primary after another and have to learn so much about the states and their different procedures and the different character of the people and all the other things that make national campaigning so complex?

ROBERT NOVAK: That has diminished over the years, particularly in the last thirty years. In the late 1950s and the early 1960s a candidate had to be careful because the mindset and the climate differed substantially from one state to another. Now there is not much difference from one state to another, contrary to much that is written and said in the media. The real differences are in the interest groups that the candidates are addressing. That is where the candidates change their positions. But the presidential candidates say almost precisely the same thing in New Hampshire that they say in Iowa or in the Southern states.

What William Kristol said suggests an anomaly today. It may not be in the spirit of the Constitution, but there are situations where people, as he said, are residents of a state almost by accident—because there were jobs there, because they wanted to live in Washington or work in the Silicon Valley. They do not belong to some established community. By a kind of accident, they are living in a community or state where they have less control over the government and less connection with the community than they have on a national level.

Since most of the states piggyback their income taxes on the federal income tax system, for example, there was a so-called windfall because tax exclusions and tax benefits but not tax rates were cut by the states. So the states had to decide whether to raise taxes for individuals or lower taxes for individuals. The debate on this issue was far removed from the individuals, far more so than the tax debate on the federal level. People who lived in Maryland got a sizable tax increase, which they did not even know about until they made out their tax forms the following year. (A minority of states got a tax cut.) This is one of the strange things that cannot be in the spirit of the Constitution, that state government seems to be farther removed than the federal government from the capability of the individual to affect it.

Mr. Ceaser: May I enter a dissent—first, as to the intentions of the framers, and, second, as to what is desirable today? The original intention of the framers is not quite so nationalist. As Madison said, "The powers delegated by the proposed Constitution to the federal government are few and defined. Those which are to remain in the state governments are numerous and indefinite."

Whatever Madison's original intention at the Constitutional Convention, the Constitution is not simply a product of Madison's mind and pen. It is the product of the convention itself. Therefore we are speaking not simply about Madison's political thought but about the U.S. Constitution, which represented a kind of compromise between two forces at the convention.

There is also the possibility that Madison himself grew to appreciate the wisdom of this position over the course of the convention. Perhaps the Madison who emerged from the convention and the Madison of subsequent years were not the same Madison who entered the convention on the first day. After all, he was involved with Thomas Jefferson and with the founding of the Democratic-Republican party, which was a defender of the states. He joined Jefferson as an author of the famous resolutions in Kentucky and Virginia, which defended the prerogatives of the states.

But to quit the mists of history and move to the present, for Mr. Kristol it seems that federal arrangements are merely a matter of convenience or, as he put it, of public policy, not a matter of juridical, constitutional separation. That is troubling because there are some positive advantages to be derived from a division of powers. That division of powers can be maintained over the long run only if it has some constitutional or juridical basis.

I do not agree with Mr. Novak on this. Different characteristics of different states are relevant and germane. The tone and character of life are certainly different in a state like Utah, where there is a powerful influence of the Mormon religion, from in a state like Massachusetts. Almost any form of regionalism, other than what is really indefensible, is worthy of being protected in this day and age, if only for the variety that it promotes.

MR. KRISTOL: Your final statement acknowledges the truth of the position that Mr. Novak and I were arguing. I happen to like regionalism as well, and the states can be a useful instrument in promoting regionalism. But that is still different from the states having a really discrete identity.

A great example is the super Tuesday presidential primary. The South is still a somewhat distinctive region, but the states within the South are not distinctive in the ways of life within them. Their all banding together—this part of the country that once was so proud of states' rights—to have a primary on one day is, in a way, a perfect example of how the particular identity of the state—the stateness of the state, the state qua state—is no longer that important.

There still is a sense that the South is different from the Northeast and that urban areas are different from rural areas. Strengthening the states, or devolving policy making down to state or local levels, will be an important way to foster the importance of states—and I am for that. But that process seems to be a kind of public policy tool rather than the early Antifederalist or states' rights vision of the states as having an individual dignity that had to be respected.

Mr. Novak finds it strange that the individual citizen has less say in the Maryland General Assembly than in the U.S. Congress, but that is consistent with the analysis of Madison that factions (we now say interest groups) are more likely to prevail at the state capital level than at the national level. Those interest groups are stronger in each of the state capitals than in the national capital, where one can at least occasionally mount a generalized campaign on behalf of the general good and overcome them.

MR. GOLDWIN: Many other nations in the world are federal in character, but all federal republics are not essentially the same. In Yugoslavia, for instance, the population in each state or republic is distinctly different from the others in ethnic character, religion, and language. They consider the federal system essential to the protection of their rights, which they think of very much as group rights.

The federal system of the United States is different from Yugoslavia's because the American states are so much like each other. That is, no single state in the Union has a majority in that state that is a minority in the nation as a whole. With a few exceptions, like Utah, the major states are microcosms of the Union as a whole.

I am not sure about the differences of the states originally—how much they differed in national origins or religion—but they probably differed more in character than they do now. That raises the possibility that over the years our federal union has had a unifying effect. In other countries, on the other hand, the federal system has a divisive effect, by maintaining and protecting the differences, and thus is an obstacle to unity. Is it possible that the federal union, even if not intended, has worked progressively to increase the unity of the nation, without destroying at least the forms of the states?

MR. KRISTOL: But it worked that way only as a result of a civil war. In the first eighty years or so it did not work terribly well to do that, and, indeed, one could argue, it went the other way. It really did require a civil war to establish the principle of the supremacy of the Union.

MR. GOLDWIN: That may be right concerning the North versus the South, or free states versus slave-owning states. But what about in the North itself? Was that process happening before the Civil War, or were the characteristics of the nonslave states distinct, and do they remain distinct?

MR. CEASER: Madison's hope was that there would be some kind of homogenization; that is spoken of in *The Federalist* as being one influence of union. After all, union did create a common market, which did not exist before, and remove the possibilities of armed conflicts among the states, which had existed. To that extent the union created a process toward removing the most peculiar kind of heterogeneities, including the expectation that it might eliminate slavery. That did not occur, but that was at least a hope of some of the framers.

MR. NOVAK: Addressing the question of whether the Constitution has a role in promoting unity or homogenization—which word is used depends on whether one looks at it favorably or unfavorably. Just in my lifetime there has been such a radical change toward homogenization that the Constitution has not had much to do with it.

Many social forces and economic forces are working here. William Kristol mentions regional differences, and there are some, but let us consider the regional differences twenty-five or thirty years ago. They were much greater than today, from both a political and an economic standpoint.

MR. CEASER: But as we become more homogeneous, it is not necessary to create institutions to promote it. The objective should be precisely the opposite. That is, in an era in which everything is moving, for other reasons, in the direction of homogenization, every effort should be bent to maintaining aspects of heterogeneity by constitutional means.

What is curious about the argument is people saying that because there are certain forces of homogenization, therefore we should look askance upon or abolish or think poorly of any idea of constitutional federalism. We should be more solicitous of federalism.

Ms. YARBROUGH: How should we go about doing that?

MR. EPSTEIN: First, Mr. Kristol's point on behalf of the states goes quite far in admitting the wisdom of the policy of preserving the states. His idea of a market, or of preserving the states as laboratories, tends to discourage despotism, to put it in the framers' terms.

What was the original purpose of having these separate states, apart from the fact that they were already there, and it was hard to eliminate them? I would recommend, in our search for the spirit of the Constitution, paying attention to the Preamble, which eloquently sums up all of the purposes of the Constitution. Among those, several, most notably defense, point quite clearly toward the Union as opposed to the states.

On the question of justice and liberty, the states can make a good claim for themselves, and perhaps also on the general welfare. But on the question of how to establish justice, there was a clear division between Madison, who believed justice is best secured by a national government because it is less subject to factious influences, and others who said we need to preserve state authority because it would be unjust to subject the people of one state to policies more appropriate to some other state.

The point about regionalism is mirrored, in a way, in the founding. This view of the importance of the states was always regarded as a kind of approximation. The states have never been so distinct or unified within themselves that one could properly say that a given group is protected if the state is autonomous because in each state there is at least some diversity, and so some do not get what they want. You will not eliminate that problem by localizing authority. That is a fundamental weakness in the antifederal position. But still it has a kind of approximate sense.

Let me turn from justice to liberty, where there is a better case for the states than justice—liberty meaning political liberty or self-government as an end in itself. With states, there are two advantages: First, there is self-government within the states, providing more opportunity for self-government. The other is that states are a check against the national government's becoming independent of the people because there are two competing governments.

The question is, How do we preserve those benefits? As the system is homogenized, and the institutions are amended, and the federal features are eroded, possibly those benefits will go too. That is why I am sympathetic to Mr. Ceaser's desire to preserve some kind of constitutional spirit in favor of preserving the states, if only for those purposes.

MR. NOVAK: Let me pose a specific issue. States' rights is a bad term, and has been for some time. Nobody uses it. But the current manifestation of states' rights is the fight by governors to maintain control over their militia, or their state national guard, which has a lot of constitutional implications. The question is, Shall these units be sent to Honduras for maneuvers with the Honduran army? This raises questions about American foreign policy.

No regional or state characteristics are involved. This is strictly a power struggle between certain governors with ideological considerations who are opposed to the foreign policy of the administration in Washington. States' rights is just a convenient pretext. This is not a grassroots issue in those states. There are no state differences; one state does not feel that it wants its national guard to be in Honduras, and another does not, because of the culture of those states. And so it has little to do with historical state rights. It is just a continuation of a party struggle with a different battleground than Washington.

MR. GOLDWIN: Are the governors of other states supporting the governors who are taking this stand?

MR. NOVAK: It depends what their position is on the foreign policy question.

MR. GOLDWIN: Are they doing it on the issue of the constitutional authority of governors over state militias?

MR. NOVAK: There might be one or two who do, but mostly it is how they stand on the foreign policy question.

MR. EPSTEIN: But this same artificiality seems evident also in the separation of powers within the national government. Not everything the legislature wants to do is distinctly related to any particular group, or related to the legislative function. In the Constitution as a whole are a number of artificial distinctions that make policy making more complicated and difficult. Part of the intention of the Constitution was to do away with the most troublesome of those complications so as to permit an energetic executive. I am not familiar enough with the details of this particular controversy, but the national government does have the authority to take command of state militias.

MR. NOVAK: The governors say that it does not under these circumstances.

MR. KRISTOL: They are wrong. But let me continue my heterodox nationalism. The founders understood, better than anyone else, the parchment barriers, as they called them: that provisions in a written constitution do not mean much without real support, real power behind them. That is the whole argument, of course, for letting "ambition check ambition" in the separation of powers.

It is just a fact that what supported state prerogatives in the past has been eroded. The income tax amendment was the most devastating blow. Once the federal government could raise revenue directly from the people, that was it for the states, except in one respect: It is important in America that governors and state legislatures are elected in visible and important elections by the people of a state because it does allow states to become vehicles for popular sentiments and movements—the tax revolt, for example—that hit the states before they hit Washington. The tax revolt took place at the local and state level and eventually was translated into policy in Washington.

In that respect the states show a real utility as a way in which we can test things in certain states. If Governor Du Pont can cut taxes and it is good for the economy in Delaware, then arguably such a thing might be wise at the national level. The states are useful, therefore, for decentralization, for experimentation in public policy, and for responsiveness to public opinion.

There is a real argument for strong states as political entities that have a realm of autonomy in which to experiment and govern. But that is quite different from the argument that was originally suggested as underlying the rationale for the states, which was the notion of shaping ways of life. That has now practically disappeared and will not be brought back.

As for Mr. Ceaser's call for strengthening the constitutional prerogatives of the states, if we favor strengthening the forces of heterogeneity and strengthening decentralization of public policy, then strengthening the states will be good in some respects. But in other respects it will be better to decentralize power to the local level, or to the individual level. Then it becomes a prudential matter of whether and how to strengthen the states rather than a constitutional issue of states' rights, or states' prerogatives vis-à-vis the federal government.

MR. CEASER: If you leave it to prudence, you have no protection. The purpose of a constitutional argument is to ensure a barrier of protection. This is the problem with justifying federalism merely on the grounds that it is a laboratory. It is a laboratory; but if you say it is merely a laboratory, then in effect your position says that the federal government can assume any power it wants, and it will agree to devolve only if it is prudentially wise and promotes some sort of laboratory. The better prudential argument is to begin with the constitutional argument, to say that here is a constitutional barrier to what the federal government can do.

MR. KRISTOL: Saying it does not make it so. What does it mean to say that there is a constitutional barrier?

MR. CEASER: We have to construct institutions that put this into effect. Education is a relevant example. Before the 1984 election we had many senators partial to federalism, even in the Democratic party, suddenly saying that because there is such a crisis in education, shouldn't the federal government begin to pay the salaries of all the teachers?

On what basis could this be resisted? Could you say that it is not prudent? The safer basis on which to resist it is to say that the care of education is constitutionally a matter for the states and localities, not for the federal government. That is the safest barrier on which to oppose this. In addition, along with just mentioning the barrier, there are mechanisms by which to put that barrier into effect.

Once governors begin to get interested in the matter of education, they will see their own career ambitions promoted by being successful in that area, as with the governor of Tennessee and the governor of Virginia. Both developed a certain pride in saying, yes, we can be the state that does the best in improving education. Once you begin to do that, you begin to develop an incentive beyond merely a parchment barrier, an incentive for the state governments themselves to insist upon their own powers.

Without some sort of incentive the parchment barriers are not enough; you get incentives by insisting on power. When everything is so confused, and no one has the responsibility, the mayors and the governors always have their hands out because there is nothing in it for them to stand up and say, we do not want this from Washington, we prefer to do it ourselves. That is what you have to build in, even if in some cases it may not be popular.

MR. NOVAK: Is the protection against this federal takeover the written Constitution?

MR. CEASER: Insisting upon the doctrine of federalism as a constitutional matter is one instrument to use against the federal takeover. It is not enough. It is also important to set in motion incentives that

13

lead governors and state legislatures to want to say, we prefer to do this ourselves rather than have a federal handout.

MR. NOVAK: I do not find any interest in that constitutional protection. There is just one reason why the hand is not out. There is no money.

MR. CEASER: That is the strongest protection today for federalism.

MR. NOVAK: It is the only protection. That is why the question of whether the "expansion of the revenue base" occurs, has great effect on the shape of the federal union. But over the years, whenever there is a problem in the states—for example, if the welfare system gets out of control—the first proposal is the federalization of welfare.

Take the so-called revenue-sharing program. The governors loved that program. I found very little pride of sponsorship over areas of government that are still controlled by the states.

MR. KRISTOL: I take a back seat to no one in applauding Governor Kean in New Jersey and Governor Alexander in Tennessee, to mention two Republican governors at random, for their efforts in education. It is healthy that they have taken initiatives whose worth can be proven and that can be imitated in other states. It is right to have incentives—though again, that is a public policy term, not a constitutional term—for them to do that. But that only proves that these days the states are useful as laboratories of restructuring, whether it is alternate certification of teachers in New Jersey, or whatever, which can then be imitated by other states.

But in the end the state of education in our nation depends much more on general developments in the national culture, a general national consensus on what children should learn, and how they should be taught it, than on discrete efforts at the state level. The discrete efforts at the state level may be useful in advancing and embodying certain reform efforts, but they are ultimately part of a national agenda and will stand or fall by whether they can succeed in carrying the day as a national agenda. Ultimately, the battle—even in education, an area where the federal role is quite limited, both in spending and in regulation—is over the soul of the nation.

Governors Kean and Alexander would say this as well. It is useful that they were able to get out ahead of the other governors, and that is why it is important to have strong states that can take the lead and do something different. But as we saw in the 1960s and 1970s, in the end the national educational system will go down or come back up as a whole.

MR. GOLDWIN: This notion of the states as laboratories means not that any good experiment they conduct will be picked up by other states but that they will become federal programs.

Mr. Kristol: They could be picked up by other states without becoming federal programs. I am simply describing how things are and how things will remain. The states are no longer fundamentally important entities. States can imitate each other. You do not need a federal program in many of these areas, and the governors, to some degree, will resist federal programs in some of these areas, although they will ask for them in others.

Mr. Ceaser: The most powerful erosion of federalism has come from the application of a uniform standard of rights through the Fourteenth Amendment to the states. The kind of discretion that would build diversity in the different units has become more and more difficult as a uniform, homogeneous notion of national rights has been imposed by the courts on the states. I would be happy to see the Supreme Court retreat from what it has been doing and allow a great deal more diversity to the states. That would be a boon for federalism.

Jack Rakove: To follow up on Mr. Ceaser's point, would it then be your line of argument that one of the ways to promote heterogeneity within the Union as a whole would be to return to the status quo ante, when states could have radically different notions of the rights appertaining to individual citizens, so that when the time came to decide whether you wanted to take a job in some state other than the one in which you were residing, a conscious element of choice would be whether your rights as a citizen, or your presumed rights as a citizen, would be better or worse protected as a consequence of that choice? Or that the rights we all would exercise would presumably be a function of state and not of federal citizenship?

Mr. Ceaser: The Constitution was changed by the Civil War amendments and by certain practices that have become precedent, but I am not radical enough to wish to overturn them. Anything that promotes heterogeneity, all things being equal, is desirable. What tends to destroy it most, besides certain interpretations of the Fourteenth Amendment, is the language of public policy because the language of public policy is not respectful of the language of law and constitution.

We should begin by insisting on the language of law and the constitution. That leaves a considerable degree of discretion to the states that it is wise to insist on. It does not bother me in the least that the character of higher education is different in Mississippi or North

Carolina from what it is in Virginia, that there are different speed limits, that one state has capital punishment and another not. And we could go on and on. That such diversity should exist does not bother me in the least. Insofar as we can create this diversity, I am not opposed to it.

Mr. Epstein: It might bother you a bit on some of those issues because on some of them there may be a right answer and a wrong answer. The constitutional principle of federalism is not necessarily identified with diversity. Suppose all of the states did the same thing. As the educational experiments were tried in the different states, and finally somebody figured out the best way to educate people, then everyone else could imitate it.

That would still be a valuable process. The idea of self-government is that one could have these decisions made by each political community; if these communities all came to the right decision, so much the better. Self-government permits states to make improvements, and it permits them to be fallible. Either way the mere fact of diversity is not the end.

Mr. Ceaser: Mere diversity is not the end, but in most instances of governing, right and wrong is not the question. On some questions of principle, it is, but there may not be one right way to educate, for example. There may be a variety of different ways consistent with different communities. In many instances governing is not finding a right way. It is finding a way that people are happy with and can live with and feel is consistent with the sort of life they want to live. To that extent, and to the extent that those ways of passing legislation do not violate fundamental rights, diversity is an end and objective. It is synonymous with the kind of liberty, the expressions of communities living the way that they want.

Mr. Goldwin: When I once visited a sixth-grade classroom in the Soviet Union, I was assured by our guide that at that very moment the same lesson was being conducted in scores of languages in sixth grades throughout the Soviet Union. I gather you would be against that, Mr. Ceaser.

Mr. Ceaser: I would, but I doubt if Mr. Epstein would be for it.

Mr. Epstein: This illustrates my point, that if you have uniformity, you may make a uniform mistake.

Mr. Kristol: Yes, to the degree there is uniformity—and there is quite a lot of it—it is because the state legislatures have insisted that all children in x state take x course in x year. That may not be a good thing, but if you really want to promote self-government of communities in the United States, more power at the state level may not be desirable. Somewhat more power at the state level might be beneficial because the state might in turn be more likely to devolve power to communities than the federal government, but that is by no means a certainty. In the field of education there has been a huge amount of centralizing and of imposing of things on local communities, precisely by state governments and state legislatures, within which certain interest groups are extremely powerful.

WALTER BERNS: I want to return to a point that Professor Yarbrough raised at the beginning, that has not been discussed. She spoke of the original expectation that the states would have something to do with promotion of the kind of moral character on which our institutions would depend.

That is true. The national government has had some effect on that. The particular instrument of this is the Supreme Court of the United States, using the Fourteenth Amendment. It is not that the states themselves were engaged in preaching, or the direct promotion of moral character, but the states, through their laws, promoted certain kinds of private institutions, for example, the family, that had this function. The original expectation was that the family would continue to exist. What we find in our own time—using the Fourteenth Amendment, and particularly the Fourteenth Amendment's equal protection clause—is the Supreme Court of the United States undermining the validity of the family. I offer one example—the failure to see the moral distinction between legitimate and illegitimate children—and ask you to comment.

MS. YARBROUGH: If I understand you correctly, I agree. The Supreme Court has undermined the original purpose of the Constitution. It is not that the state constitutions themselves necessarily took an active role. In some cases they did, as in the New England constitutions. But they were friendly to the proposition that a moral people is the best preserve of republican institutions. This concern with character manifested itself differently in different states. Moreover people were divided within states over whether religion or education was more efficacious in forming republican character.

And people were also divided, when they talked about education, about the proper function of education. Everyone agreed that it was to promote good citizenship, but they disagreed on how one went about doing that. The Jeffersonians believed that it was done best through the study of history and a secular education. The non-Jeffersonians believed that this was done best through a religious education. After the Constitution was ratified, a variety of proposals was put forth by prominent citizens who consciously sought to complete the framers' project. One of the things missing in this discussion is the sense that the spirit of the Constitution has to include the spirit of the original state constitutions. The federal Constitution is, in some sense, incomplete. And so I dissent from Professor Epstein's insistence that we look simply to the Preamble of the federal Constitution because if we look there and not to the state constitutions, we do not find any of these purposes taken up.

Now that the states are no longer permitted these activities, mostly as a result of Supreme Court rulings, the question is, Do we now consider these purposes unnecessary or obsolete? Do they now become functions of the national government, or where do we take them? Are we simply concerned with the spirit of the Constitution as set forth in the Preamble, or is there another aspect to this spirit? When we look at federalism, we must look at that part of the federal system that is not included in the federal Constitution, and that is the state constitutions.

MR. BERNS: That point was raised and defended by the members of the first Congress, when they were debating the Bill of Rights, and in particular the First Amendment. That point of view is ignored altogether in the modern Supreme Court when these questions come up under the equal protection clause, and that is a matter of real concern.

MR. KRISTOL: I yield only to Walter Berns in my dislike of many modern Supreme Court decisions. But it is not clear that state governments have always been friendly to the family or to the family role in education. The state of Oregon tried to prohibit families from sending their children to religious schools; that was overturned in 1925 by the Supreme Court, in *Pierce* v. *Society of Sisters,* on grounds of individual rights.

On the issue of legitimacy and illegitimacy, the Court decisions were not necessarily correct, but again it does seem that at heart there was a national change in the culture. To reverse that would require a national reversal of certain cultural assumptions and norms, rather than simply an appeal to federalism. That is, speaking politically, federalism may be part of a means toward reversing certain movements and tendencies and decisions, but it does not seem to be sufficient. Today, speaking politically, I am not persuaded that an appeal to federalism as a grand principle in opposition to all these developments is likely to be successful.

MR. BERNS: One can say that at the state level there was less appreciation of liberty, understood not as self-government but as being left alone. For the defense of liberty so understood, we depend upon the Supreme Court of the United States. But, equally valid, at the state level there was more appreciation of the necessity of concern for character and morality, the sort of thing Professor Yarbrough was talking about, and much less appreciation at the national level. There has to be a balance here.

CHARLES FAIRBANKS: This discussion has left out what, most of all, has undermined federalism, and what is also the determining factor in the way we inevitably view the future of federalism. What kind of diversity was federalism used to defend? Above all it defended the institution of slavery, with its heritage, an institution that denied the blessings of liberty to a large part of the population.

It seems that federalism is now so weak because federalism was used to defend slavery and the aftermath of slavery. That is what discredited federalism to a great degree with people who did not believe in those institutions. In the South, where in my childhood the belief in federalism was really quite strong, it is still a living thing. This transition to the world in which there was no longer a strong drive toward federalism, toward taking federalism seriously, results from the South eventually giving up on defending racial inequality after *Brown* v. *Board of Education*.

Could the people who want to keep alive the heritage of federalism address how we ought to view that experience?

MS. YARBROUGH: First of all, in a biracial society with slavery, there is racism, there is prejudice, there is discrimination, regardless of the kind of political system. We can point to other countries in the world that are not federal systems and also discriminate against their peoples on the basis of race. The larger question is not the question of federalism, but the question of what to do in a biracial society where one race was brought in slavery.

That would have been a difficult question to solve, whether we had federalism or not. As it turned out, federalism then is bound up with any solution or difficulty, but it is not the cause of the difficulty. The cause of the difficulty is the attempt to establish, for the first time in human history, a biracial society in which minorities enjoy the same protections and freedoms as the majority. That is the much greater question.

There is also a tendency to confuse federalism with states' rights. One of the beneficial outcomes of the Fourteenth Amendment was establishing that there are certain things the states cannot do. I do not think that Professor Ceaser and I in any way wish to go back, to turn the clock back to a pre–Civil War society, to countenance any sort of discrimination against blacks or any other people. The national government has the principal responsibility for guaranteeing the rights of minorities, but there is still room for enormous diversity on other issues where the fundamental rights of all Americans are not in question.

MR. NOVAK: The interest in federalism in the South died with the political revolution in the South, which did not occur instantly with *Brown* v. *Board of Education* but did occur after the civil rights revolution of the 1960s.

People who do not live in the South are way behind the knowledge curve on how much politics has changed there. Southern public opinion and the way Southern senators voted on the Bork confirmation case were a dramatic and shocking illustration of that. And I find no greater interest in the theoretical concept of federalism, or the reserve powers of the states, shown by Southern governors, compared to governors anyplace else.

There might be some difference on federalism issues between Republican governors and Democratic governors, whether they are in the North or South, but not much difference. They are much closer to each other than Republican members of Congress are to Democratic members of Congress. There is much more bipartisanship. But with the settlement of the race question in the South—so that it at least is as settled as in the North—much of the interest in the political structure for maintaining and discussing federalism has disappeared.

PATRICIA WALD: We have talked about the conflict in instances when the federal courts or in some cases Congress has overriden or told the states that they must bring rights up to a certain level, or they cannot exclude people, and also has established a floor, in many cases, as to what the states could do. But the states do appear to be active in interpreting their constitutions to enlarge rights. In other words they have taken rights above and beyond what the federal courts and the Supreme Court have declared them to be.

One of the most interesting areas is criminal justice. Many interpretations of state constitutions have increased rights under the Fourth Amendment of search and seizure or the state counterpart. The Supreme Court has taken the view that if a state supreme court declares a right, it had better be clear that it is declaring a right under the state constitution, not under the federal. Otherwise the Supreme Court presumes that the right is under the federal Constitution and rules by the federal doctrine. Many states have taken the signal and have been explicit, in their constitutions and in their interpretations, in enlarging rights, not exclusively in the criminal area, but in other areas as well. Thereby they do appear to be making an impact over and above the homogenization or the federalization occurring in other areas.

MR. EPSTEIN: The desirability of that process depends quite a bit on whether the state courts or the state legislatures are enlarging these rights. It seems entirely within the state legislatures' prerogative to do anything they want about criminal law, as long as they have not violated the floor of rights. But for state courts to invent new rights, is an infection from the national example.

Ms. WALD: The state constitutions are the governing charter of the state legislatures. The state courts are still presumed to be the exclusive interpreter of state constitutions. If they interpret their state constitutions to provide those rights, is that illegitimate?

MR. CEASER: If they interpret their state constitutions in the same way that some federal judges interpret the Constitution of the United States, there might be a problem. The question is not merely one of where powers are located but also one of self-government. Are we moving too much into an era in which decisions of public policy are made by courts rather than legislatures? The legitimate province of the courts is interpreting what law is and what law means. Where state courts genuinely interpret state constitutions, there is a proper role. Where state courts engage in creative interpretations of state constitutions, that is, writing into the state constitutions what they like, we have the same problem at the state level that we have at the federal level.

JUDGE WALD: Isn't that a different debate?

MR. CEASER: It certainly is a different debate. Justice Brennan, for example, suggested that the action should move now from the federal courts to the state courts. He was afraid that the federal courts might actually begin looking at the Constitution more carefully and not reading new rights into it. He invited his colleagues at the state level to start reading the state constitutions creatively, as a way of getting into the living body of America what he considers to be more rights.

But I am not always clear that these are extensions of rights. They are extensions of someone's conceptions of rights, often at the expense of others' conceptions of rights.

JUDGE WALD: But isn't that a part of federalism? In a sense a part of federalism is a state court system interpreting its own state law. We may not like the results, although one interesting thing about state constitutions is that they can be amended or repealed or completely changed much easier than the federal Constitution.

MR. CEASER: The judges are also subject, in many states, to expulsion from the courts.

BENJAMIN BARBER: We have not yet addressed directly the question of the heterogeneity that the federal system provides as against the uniformity that standards of justice and rights require. It does not seem adequate to respond to that dilemma, as perhaps Jean Yarbrough did, by simply bracketing the Fourteenth Amendment and a biracial society and saying once that has been established, from then on, heterogeneity can prevail. It seems that almost all of the issues, including the ones debated a moment ago, are really issues that involve a controversy about what constitutes a universal standard, what constitutes a right.

And it seems difficult to argue that the principle of heterogeneity can be utilized across the board, to say simply that states ought to be permitted, except in one or two cases, to do as they please. I can imagine a whole series of areas, and the Supreme Court in fact has defined such areas in the last forty or fifty years, that seemed to imply uniform standards of justice and require national regulation, *Roe* v. *Wade*, for example. So the heterogeneous principle seems a much thornier problem, and one that is much more difficult to get around. It is fraught with difficulty for anybody interested in defending justice and rights for individuals.

Mr. Epstein: It is a problem if one formulates the tension as between justice or rights, on the one hand, and heterogeneity, on the other. In that case who is to speak up for heterogeneity as against the truth or rights?

But the central virtue of federalism is not heterogeneity but self-government: human beings acting as political communities and ruling themselves. This was the great argument for more local governments—that such political activity is possible, that government is closer to the people.

The virtues of self-government are many and would have to be discussed separately, but self-government is really what is at stake. Federalism is in tension with the universal standard of justice or truth but also an obstacle to universal standard of error or to despotism or tyranny.

The belief is that self-government is what makes one wish not simply to embrace the standard of truth, and makes one reluctant to say, "If it's best, then everyone should do it." That reluctance on behalf of self-government recommends federalism.

Mr. Goldwin: If it seems that this discussion has not given one clear and unified answer to the question but rather a diversity of answers that nevertheless have some cohesion, perhaps that outcome, for this topic, is entirely fitting.

2
Commerce

ROBERT GOLDWIN: The United States is a commercial society, however else it might be described. The Constitution in numerous ways acknowledges the commercial character of the nation and the people. As one president of the United States said some time ago, "The business of America is business." And as James Madison wrote, "The protection of different and unequal faculties of acquiring property is the first object of government."

Most of us consider commerce important and perhaps even vital, but most of us do not consider commerce lofty or noble. Gangsters fight and die over business deals, but few of us nongangsters consider commerce a cause worth dying for. And yet commerce seems to be essential to liberty and security of rights as well as to prosperity. It is difficult to think of any free society, anywhere in the world, where civil rights are secure, that is not also a commercial society. Did the founders seek to constitute a commercial society, and if so, what did they have in mind, and to what extent, and in what ways, can it be said that commerce is the spirit of the Constitution?

MORTON FRISCH: While the restructuring of the American regime was surely done with a view to enhancing commerce, and while many passages in the Constitution clearly reflect this intention, the spirit of the Constitution is not adequately explained or even well-explained by the acquisitive spirit. If the spirit of the Constitution could be explained or defined in terms of the acquisitive spirit then so could the Articles of Confederation. Therefore, what is distinctive about the American Constitution must be looked for somewhere else. What is the distinctiveness of the American Constitution?

Montesquieu pointed out that a free society requires not only the freedom of the constitution, accomplished through separation of powers and checks and balances, but also the freedom of the individual, or civil rights. In other words a society is not truly free according to Montesquieu merely if the forms are republican, for the forms, despite John Locke's hope, are not an adequate substitution for individual rights. Montesquieu did not believe that liberty can be protected simply by institutional arrangements.

The American Constitution—and this is its distinctiveness—combines the freedom of the constitution with that of the individual. This was done even before the Bill of Rights was incorporated into the Constitution, as Alexander Hamilton pointed out in *Federalist* No. 84: no ex post facto laws, no bills of attainder, prohibition against suspension of the privilege of writ of habeas corpus. One could say that the passage of the Bill of Rights underscored and enhanced this synthesis. To characterize the spirit of the Constitution as the acquisitive spirit, a spirit that was surely present in the Constitution but is not its hallmark principle, is in effect to accept the analysis of Charles Beard.

ROGER STARR: First of all, I disagree with the use of the phrase "the acquisitive spirit." It seems that commerce represents something other than or besides or in addition to the acquisitive spirit. It means not only that men and women have an interest in the acquisition of property but also that they have an interest in communication and intercourse regarding that property. One of the important elements of the Constitution that appears in the enumerated powers is the protection of intercourse of a commercial nature. This was of great importance to the writers of the Constitution because this was to be one of the elements that would unify the thirteen individual colonies into a single society, whether it be the unity of a central government or the unity of a federal government.

If the thirteen colonies had each existed only on agriculture—which some of the founding fathers certainly regarded as important to a republican society—the emphasis would have been on individuality and the lack of commerce between the parts. But the emphasis was on the building of post roads, and even on such things as permission for states to enter into compacts with each other, from which we have developed such things as the Port Authority of New York and New Jersey, which has had a tremendous effect on an interstate harbor system and has been important in the relationship between these two states. These things have had a marked impact or a marked demonstration of the spirit of emerging unity, which seems basic to the Constitution.

MARK PLATTNER: In reply to Professor Frisch's statement, first, no one would claim that commerce is the exclusive spirit or the principal animating spirit of the Constitution. To acknowledge that, however, is in no way sufficient to deny that commerce is one of the important elements of the spirit of the Constitution. Second, as to whether the Constitution, as opposed to the Articles of Confederation, in some way provides more for a commercial society or assumes a commercial society, the proof of that is really in *Federalist* No. 10. The whole scheme of the extended republic proposed by James Madison presupposes a society with a diversity of interests, which can be brought about only in a commercial society. A simple agricultural society would not provide the diversity required by the scheme of *Federalist* No. 10.

MR. FRISCH: But there already was a commercial society under the Articles of Confederation, which was a unified society. The constitutional system may not have accommodated it as well as it should, but it seems that it was already in existence.

LAURENCE SILBERMAN: Two points troubled me about Mr. Frisch's initial statement. First, he distinguishes the freedom of the individual from the acquisitive spirit. Doesn't individual freedom include the freedom to acquire material goods? Isn't that part of it? Second, by equating commerce with the acquisitive spirit, are you not doing a disservice to the notion of commerce? It is like equating national defense with the aggressive spirit. That is to say, commerce may well be based, in part, on individual acquisitiveness, but is not commerce a good deal bigger, more important, more complex, and different from the acquisitive spirit?

MR. FRISCH: I do not see how it is bigger or more complex. There is nothing wrong with the acquisitive spirit, and commerce at its best reflects the acquisitive spirit.

HARVEY FLAUMENHAFT: Speaking in terms of acquisition attends to one side of something with two sides. Acquisition as such is not in the public interest. Acquisition of a certain sort is thought to be good for the public. An epitome of the attitude of the founders toward commerce is to be found in the only clause in the Constitution that mentions a right and gives a purpose for the power that it grants. Article I, section 8, deals with patents and copyrights. There the Constitution says that to promote the progress of science and useful arts, Congress has the power to grant an exclusive right to authors and inventors for a limited time.

That is an epitome of the issue because it is an exclusive right, and it has to do with acquisition, but it has a stated purpose, and the exclusive right is given for a limited time. This section seems to recognize that there is good in allowing people to benefit themselves, and there is some good in so arranging things so that their benefiting themselves is not in conflict with their benefiting others. That is acquisition of a sort.

AMY BRIDGES: When I first thought about this issue, I thought that the spirit of commerce could perhaps be the spirit of the charter of the East India Company or of the founding documents of Merrill Lynch, but surely not of the Constitution. In fact *The Federalist* argues that republicanism is the spirit of the Constitution. But the founders were also concerned about creating a frame of government appropriate to the genius of the people and to their situation. On both counts commerce was central to their project. Certainly by the time Tocqueville got to the United States, there was constant talking and debating about political economy, about commerce, about how it works, about the place of the United States in the world, and about the relationship of different people in the United States to one another in its domestic commerce.

The founders were extremely farsighted about the economy and the shape that it was going to assume. Hamilton argued about the importance of commerce for the liberty of Americans vis-à-vis Europe, and he saw a world economic system in which the United States would be imperialized, as it were, by Europe, not just because Europeans were better armed and had standing armies and navies that dwarfed our own but also because they were commercially superior to the United States. And so in his vision the United States needed to grow to avoid becoming a victim of the European powers. That was at the heart of his project and the Constitution.

MR. GOLDWIN: There seems to be a powerful connection between the commercial spirit and the liberties that are somewhat loftier and more praiseworthy. But still there is this strange—and universal—fact that without commerce there is no liberty. I do not know of examples of noncommercial societies where there is also political liberty. Now there are some commercial societies where rights are not very secure, but they usually are nations that were previously not commercial, that are now becoming commercial; as they become commercial, they find it harder to deny security of individual rights.

There is something profound about commerce that is more than private acquisition and selfishness. There is some relationship between commerce and liberty that a constitution maker who cares about liberty has to take into account.

MR. STARR: In eighteenth-century Europe land was an essential element of liberty. Some of the people who were actually in attendance when the Constitution was being written were themselves deeply involved in the speculative purchase of land beyond the frontiers of the colonies, or at the edges, including George Washington and James Wilson from Pennsylvania. The land represented freedom to the people of Europe. The desire to have land of one's own was probably one of the great supports of the whole notion of human liberty. It was not only an abstract idea, it was a very concrete idea. To develop that land it was necessary to develop a commercial enterprise that would pay for the costs of the land development.

Washington, according to James T. Flexner's biography, was

deeply concerned with trying to develop a canal boat that effectively would go uphill so that his lands in what is now West Virginia could be developed. Nobody could afford to build such a boat, even if it could have been invented, without commercial enterprise. One cannot separate commerce from the availability of land and its usefulness to the people.

Mr. Plattner: Bob Goldwin's correlation between commerce and liberty is true if one interprets liberty in the sense of private rights and the security of private rights, as opposed to liberty in the sense of self-government. Among the ancient republics Sparta is perhaps the most extreme example of a society that forbids commerce altogether, but for thousands of years it was regarded as a model of self-government.

It was a model, however, that the framers of the American Constitution clearly rejected. What they had in mind was a system that provided for the security of private rights, the rights of individuals against their government, and in that connection there is an obvious link with commerce and the security of private property.

Mr. Silberman: I am not sure that the framers ever contemplated the kind of theoretical attack by various doctrines on private property and indeed on commercial society that we have seen in the twentieth century. To be sure, there was Sparta, and there were certain feudal societies. But the founders never visualized the kind of doctrinal attack on the commercial society that would have led them to make the connection explicitly for which Mr. Goldwin is searching, although they probably had it implicitly in mind. But one does not have to think about that connection very hard if nobody is attacking it.

Mr. Flaumenhaft: In reading Hamilton's defense of his financial policies, it becomes clear that there is quite a bit of suspicion of the commercial spirit, although maybe not an attack on property as such. After all, what we are talking about is not property as such but a certain kind of property and a certain kind of economy that did not just come into being by itself. The economy had to be promoted by effort and choice and argument. Quite a few people did not want it to come into being, including some people who are sometimes thought of as founding fathers.

Mr. Silberman: You make a point there. But isn't it fair to say that although a number of the framers explicitly worried about the potential redistribution efforts of a majority in a particular government—whether state or federal—there was never any concern about the kind of onslaught on capitalism that we see in the twentieth century? Therefore, they did not explicitly think about liberty and capitalism.

Mr. Flaumenhaft: On the contrary capitalism took some doing

to come into being. Thomas Jefferson and his friends, for instance, wanted to strangle it in its cradle. Capitalism did not come into being in a fit of absentmindedness. It had to be worked for.

Ms. BRIDGES: But there also was a mercantile theory against the sort of liberty that we associate with property. It was a full-blown ideology, which said that the sort of thing you are talking about is a crazy idea, that the whole world will come apart and we will just have anarchy if people can barter and exchange as they want.

MR. SILBERMAN: That is a fair point. Certainly Adam Smith, with whom all the framers were familiar, had attacked mercantilism. But that is something different from what we are talking about now. Smith suggested that there was some link between political liberty and a freer economy. But Hamilton and Jefferson differed in terms of what kind of commercial activity would be preferred. After all, when Jefferson described commercial activity, he was using commerce as somehow different from an agricultural economy.

MR. FRISCH: Everybody understands the relationship between property and freedom. We also know that acquisitiveness is a higher principle than greed. But it seems that the question of the spirit of the Constitution now can be turned into another question: Is property serving freedom or is freedom in the service of property?

MR. PLATTNER: One would not say that freedom is in the service of property. Certainly one would state it the other way around. But I would not minimize the extent to which prosperity, let us say, was viewed as an end of the political order, both by the framers and certainly by us today. And no politician is going to stay in office very long if he does not produce economic policies that are successful.

MR. FLAUMENHAFT: To talk about the progress of science and useful arts is not to talk only about the prerequisites of liberty. It is also to talk about prosperity and enterprise.

MR. FRISCH: But the question that was raised is to what extent commerce reflects the spirit of the Constitution.

MR. PLATTNER: It is an essential ingredient, although not the culmination or the goal of the constitutional system.

MR. FRISCH: That is what I was trying to say also. We already had a commercial society before the Constitution. The political order was not in synch with that commercial society.

MR. GOLDWIN: Right. There were obviously a lot of obstacles. That is why they were calling conventions and had tried once or twice before Philadelphia, because there were obstacles to commerce.

MR. FRISCH: Passages in the Constitution reflect a commercial emphasis, but we are asking to what extent this reflects the spirit of the Constitution. Is this the dominating spirit? Is this the distinctiveness of the American Constitution? We already had a constitution that reflected the spirit of commerce because it was a commercial society.

MR. STARR: That is a double-edged argument because if we already had it, and it worked so well, why did we have a new Constitution? The existing constitution was not working. I cannot tell whether we have an 80-proof Constitution or a 40-proof Constitution. But the men who wrote this Constitution felt that without economic prosperity liberty would not survive very long, neither individual liberty nor the liberty of the colonies as a whole. And therefore it is a part of the essential spirit. Certainly not all they did in Philadelphia was to develop incorporation papers. They did more than that. But commerce was and is part of the essence of the Constitution.

MR. SILBERMAN: If one takes a step back and looks at the period immediately before the Constitutional Convention, it is perfectly apparent that the delegates did not come to Philadelphia because of any external threat. That is to say, they did not form an effective, central government under a Constitution because they were worried—as they might well otherwise have been—about an attack from England or France or any other foreign power. Nor did they seem to come together largely because of political reasons. Ninety percent of the reason for their meeting in Philadelphia was indeed commercial—the continued annoyance with the barriers to trade interposed by one colony against the other, one state against the other. If one looks at the legislative history—the reason for coming to Philadelphia—it was 90 percent commercial in the sense of interstate commerce.

MR. FRISCH: What about impressment of our sailors on the high seas? What about states making treaties with foreign nations? Weren't they considerations?

MR. SILBERMAN: The states making treaties with foreign nations was a concern only in commercial terms. No one at that time was worried about any state making a political alliance with a foreign nation. It is true that when the delegates came to Philadelphia and started to debate various structures of the Constitution, the thought occurred, but that was not a clear-and-present danger. What they were concerned about, primarily—in fact there was more discussion of this than anything else—was the fact that New York and Pennsylvania were being rotten to New Jersey in terms of exports. And that was a problem about which many states were worried.

MR. FRISCH: It seems that Judge Silberman is identifying the coming into being, or the condition of a thing, with the essence, or the being of a thing. Simply because existing problems motivated the founders to go to the Annapolis convention, and ultimately, to the

Philadelphia convention, that condition, or that coming into being, does not necessarily characterize the peculiarity or the distinctiveness of the final product.

The distinctiveness of the American Constitution is that it did exactly what Montesquieu said a truly free society ought to do, and that is to combine the freedom of the Constitution with the freedom of the individual. The American Constitution was the first constitution to do this. And that does not mean that the acquisitive spirit, which is a very fine spirit, is not in alliance with that freedom and does not serve that freedom because it certainly does.

JACK RAKOVE: This kind of discussion makes historians like myself very nervous. The loose bandying about of historical context makes me wince. Let me report on two sets of historical facts. One relates to the larger question of how one conceptualizes commerce. The discussion to this point has been unsatisfactory because it is not clear whether we think of commerce as the simple protection of rights of property and acquisition, or mechanisms of exchange, and the creation of conditions leading to sustained economic growth and prosperity.

We should first think about the context within which the constitution is being framed. Historians have been debating for some years now the question of how one characterizes the nature of economic ambitions in late eighteenth-century America.

There are certainly those who look to Hamilton as the spokesman for a kind of Adam Smith–like notion of how in fact commerce, and the creation of wealth, can lead to sustained economic growth and prosperity. And a whole other school, mostly on the left—Marxist, neo-Marxist, or quasi-Marxist—looks to the idea that although rights of property are certainly important in this society, the goal of acquiring property was not to promote economic growth as we think about it in the capitalistic sense, but rather the preservation of the independence of the freeholder or the urban artisan who aspires to something comparable within his own place in the economic system.

There is a need to try to work out a hierarchy of economic motives that will somehow embrace the concerns of the Hamiltonians, which are very forward-looking in terms of figuring America's place in a world system and creating conditions of sustained growth, and to juxtapose those concerns with the somewhat more moderate positions of Jefferson and Madison. They saw Americans as a vigorous, enterprising people, but the purpose of their economic activity may not be the creation of a fully developed, modern, capitalist state but rather a more mixed economy.

The second point is a comment on what has been said and not said. Although there is much that Judge Silberman said with which I do not agree, to some extent he is closer than anybody else in terms of trying to get the background of the convention.

You really have not identified the most important issue that precedes the politics of 1787. It is one that has become fairly obscure to most of us today: the closure of the Mississippi to American navigation at New Orleans by the Spanish, which, in the calculations of people like Madison and James Wilson, was a very serious problem. There was a great shift of population westward: people settling the Ohio Valley in a kind of unregulated flow of settlement. Everyone knew that these people would look for outlets for the produce that they would begin to raise. If they could not get it out, and if the existing federal government could not somehow get access for American goods down to the Gulf of Mexico, the United States would lose control of the interior of the continent, and would not control the lands it has acquired by the Treaty of Paris. And therefore loyalties in the interior would shift to some kind of accommodation with the Spanish. This recognition of the export potential of the interior, the desire of these kind of yeoman farmers moving West, the expectation that eventually they would be producing surpluses that they would want to market, that testifies—even for the Jeffersonians and the Madisonians—to the acceptance of a certain kind of acquisitiveness on the part of the agrarian population.

Whether that kind of acquisitiveness can be linked with the kind of protocapitalistic notions of commerce in the Hamiltonian sense remains a great puzzle and a great problem. But one has to try to conceptualize and clarify the range of economic ambitions that existed in an economy that was in intense transition. This discussion has skipped over this.

Mr. Goldwin: On the groundwork you have just laid, to what extent do you think commerce is the spirit of the Constitution?

Mr. Rakove: There is no doubt that most of the framers went to Philadelphia determined to place a national economy on a much more sensible footing than existed under the Articles of Confederation. And if we reconstruct the history of the various schemes to amend the articles, back to 1781, especially to 1783, the addition of commercial powers to the existing delegation of powers to the confederation was paramount.

On that basis alone, one must say that a concern with creating the conditions for a common market at home and improving the position of America vis-à-vis other nations is certainly fundamental to the

31

whole enterprise. Whether the idea that commercial people will be good citizens, the idea that man pursuing rational self-interested behavior will provide what might be called the moral basis of a republic, is an argument that has not been raised so far. But many of us know that it is also very much a part of the discussion of eighteenth-century thought.

JOSEPH CROPSEY: Mr. Goldwin's question is singularly well put, it seems to me, because it is so hard to answer.

To what extent is the United States Constitution animated by a spirit of commerce, or how much of the commercial principle accounts for the spirit of the United States Constitution? Part of the difficulty of answering this question lies in the fact that there is something defective about the term "commercial society"; that was at least suggested by Amy Bridges's remark about mercantilism. A mercantilist society is a kind of commercial society. This leads me, parenthetically, to respond to what Judge Silberman said about the unusualness of reservations about a commercial society, or the property principle, however "commercial society" is to be understood. Rather the opposite is the case when one stops to think about it. Reservations about property, from one point of view or another, have been expressed as far back as Plato, and steadily by Christianity. All sorts of books had to be written about what overcame the principle of traditional Catholic Christianity in the interest of capitalism, to give the commercial principle a chance. The expression of mercantilism is a kind of reservation against that. That reservation is found even in such people as Rousseau.

The principle of commercial freedom had in its own way the task of the scow that was going to go uphill; it was an uphill fight. The principle of the U.S. Constitution is at least to some extent affected by the arguments of Adam Smith. That tendency is of course in favor of one kind of capitalism, or one kind of property principle, against another. Adam Smith is relevant in this case. His notion was that property is in the service of freedom because otherwise the principle of property carried such heavy adverse moral freight that it could hardly be justified if something very good, higher than itself, did not follow from it. Smith is famous for illustrating a moral problem raised by the emancipation of the principle of acquisition, of antimercantilism.

As far as the American Constitution is animated by a laissez-faire commercial principle, it is so in the face of certain moral problems that were perceived to accompany the emancipation of that principle for the sake of the freedom of the individual, in which respect the Constitution is probably in the spirit of Locke. People who use the term "commercial society" probably ought to do it in comprehension of the fact that there were at least two kinds of commercial society known to people in that time, and the Constitution probably, as far as it is a Smith-like document, inclines toward one rather than consciously against the other one, and therefore in favor of private rights.

MR. SILBERMAN: There is one respect in which the Constitution clearly leans toward Adam Smith and against mercantilism. It is indeed the very point that was the single greatest cause of the convention: to break down barriers to interstate commerce. And those barriers are simply a form of mercantilism. In that respect the notion was adopted. You are quite right that private property has faced attacks going back as far as Plato.

I was making a somewhat different point. When Bob Goldwin raises the question, Is the Constitution animated by a spirit of commercialism? he seems to be raising a question that is almost more relevant for the twentieth than the eighteenth and early nineteenth centuries. That was the only point I was making.

What the framers did adopt in the Constitution was what they thought was the protection against the dangers with which they were most concerned. Those dangers were barriers to interstate commerce. Those dangers were an arrogation of federal power. They did not seem to be animated by a fear, or a threat, to commercialism except insofar as it would reflect itself in mercantilism, not as it has reflected itself by doctrines of the twentieth century.

MR. GOLDWIN: If you mean that Marxism did not exist in their time, then I would agree. But otherwise the prejudices or sentiments against anything we would now consider commercial were powerful from ancient times on philosophic grounds, on religious grounds, and even as a matter of taste. The landowners of the seventeenth and eighteenth centuries also sneered at commerce as not a high human activity.

HERMAN BELZ: Professor Rakove was expressing a little frustration at the inattention to history. The problem of virtue should be brought in here. Whom are we arguing against? Everybody agrees that the commercial spirit is part of the founding generation. The other side of the problem that we need to talk a bit about is the argument that the Constitution is perhaps founded on virtuous regard for the good of the whole. This leads to the Antifederalist, perhaps defending that point of view, and the Federalist, speaking for individual rights, natural rights, and commercial activity.

To present a fuller picture of what the historians and political scientists are arguing about, I ask a couple of questions. To what extent is the Constitution based on the commercial spirit? How can one answer that in quantitative terms? Of course we do not need a quantitative answer, but that is partly at issue. Was the civic-minded republicanism the decisive factor in the founding of institutions, or should the commercial spirit, the commercial activity be recognized more? Since the Federalists wrote the Constitution and prevailed, they would have an edge in deciding this issue.

Ms. BRIDGES: However commercial we decide the Constitution was, or was not, many issues were unresolved. Was the idea of being a chartered corporation, for example, an exercise in property rights, or was it the granting of an unfair privilege to some people when other people did not have it and so a violation of the idea that government should shower its favors equally on all its citizens?

But if we look at the work of the social historians, many of whom are left-leaning, the picture is one in which popular political culture is very much taken up with the commercial spirit after all.

MR. PLATTNER: If one looks at people like Jefferson who in some sense were opposed to commerce, it is nonetheless very clear that in their view of private property, of the desire for gain, they were essentially Lockean. The whole American debate was already fundamentally beyond that older debate about whether the desire for acquisition was legitimate and so on. It took place within a context that accepted that desire; the agrarian position was already somewhat compromised in that respect.

MR. FLAUMENHAFT: Jefferson was the man who said if ever God had a chosen people, they are the farmers because they are not dependent on other people; they are not primarily buyers and sellers but rely on their own labor, and the rain from above. Let us keep the workshops in the cities. He might have been committed in some way to property and acquisition, and to Locke, but there was a limit to that.

MR. PLATTNER: But he also spoke about how every man should be rewarded with the fruits of his own labor, and how those whose fathers have labored more successfully deserve to get the additional rewards that that labor brings.

MR. FLAUMENHAFT: He was ambivalent because he wanted to have his cake and eat it.

WILLIAM ALLEN: In a fairly simple-minded approach to the original question, and therefore the discussion, there was no more common truth during the founding period than every man under his own vine and fig tree. That fairly well sums up the popular as well as the reflective attitude toward property rights, and does not necessarily translate into any kind of economic system.

To interpret the question as asking whether one or the other economic system is the spirit of the Constitution is perhaps a mistake.

34

We can take James Madison as a witness. The opening comments quoted Madison as saying that the first object of government is the protection of the diverse faculties of human beings. He also said that the principal task of modern legislation is the regulation of these various and interfering interests, all of which happen to be economic, and commercial. Once one goes through his description of these interests, one sees they appear only in commercial societies. The manufacturing interests he discussed are not present in an agricultural society. So Madison answers the question: commerce is entirely involved with the spirit of the Constitution. We cannot separate them.

The founding generation altogether answers it that way. In 1758, Nathaniel Ames, who was the premier almanac writer of the century for about fifty years continuously, published a prediction of a continentwide union as a condition of American political prosperity. And that continentwide union included descriptions of economic activities—mining, building of great cities, manufacturing—that were common through the era. Now no one can contemplate that kind of life—as so many did in that era—without contemplating commerce as the integral and inherent aspect of their lives. That is the most direct answer to the question, which then raises only theoretical problems for us.

JEAN YARBROUGH: I feel called upon to vindicate the honor of the political scientists to my colleague and friend, Jack Rakove. One issue that has emerged somewhat but not sufficiently was suggested by Judge Silberman. The country as a whole was a commercial society; the debate was over the kind of commercial activity. It is a mistake to take Jefferson in one place, in the "Notes on Virginia," where he said that we need to have these self-sufficient independent farmers, and read into it a Jeffersonian alternative for America that was some kind of Arcadia where each man had his little farm and was a self-sufficient farmer in some classic yeoman sense.

That is not the case at all. A fuller study of Jefferson would confirm, and historians have certainly shown, that he was as much a commercial thinker as Hamilton, but he had in mind a different kind of commercial activity. His desire that these farmers in the new Western territories would participate in international markets by marketing their excess crops was not exactly the self-sufficient farmer that one generally pictures.

Both sides were concerned with a commercial spirit, but they saw a different kind of commercial activity as appropriate for republican institutions. Both of them were concerned with the moral effects of the kind of commercial activity that they hoped to encourage. Oddly enough, when Jefferson and Hamilton talked about the sorts of vir-

35

tues that they expected their commercial enterprise to generate, both were largely in agreement that these were the virtues of frugality, industry, and self-development and that these virtues were appropriate to a commercial republic rather than to a martial, slave-holding classical republic.

Mr. FLAUMENHAFT: Jefferson was not noncommercial at bottom. Some of his statements that are often quoted are utterly at odds with other things he said and acted upon; that was the character of much of his thinking.

The real question is whether people with his vision of commerce in America appreciated the dynamic quality of commerce. Did unrealistic views lead them to try to keep commerce from becoming fully commerce?

EDWARD BANFIELD: Benjamin Franklin epitomizes the commercial spirit. After all he was the man who wanted to give us the turkey instead of the eagle as a national symbol. In his autobiography he told us that in his early years he read Locke's "Essay concerning Human Understanding," and he apparently was very much taken with Locke's account of the importance and the rationality of morality. In fact in the autobiography he described his youthful plan for making himself perfect, which reflects Locke's views very well. In the essay Locke wrote that man is endowed by his Creator with a rational faculty sufficient to get him a long way toward—not all the way perhaps—true happiness, which is the end of existence. But he added there, as in almost every other similar passage, "if he will only use it"—and it turns out that man does not use it in a great majority of cases. And although Locke did not say so explicitly, it is clear that he thought man ought to use it. Otherwise why write as he did in his book on education that it is a great obligation to induce by example, or otherwise, rationality to children at the earliest possible point?

It is clear that Locke deplored the irrational person who remained poor when he could, by the use of his God-given faculties, make himself a little money and get ahead in the world and provide for his comfort and well-being and long life. Without turning him into a Benjamin Franklin, Locke clearly thought that there were such things as higher pleasures, and that the faculty of reason was sufficient to cultivate them. Men could attain to higher and more virtuous levels in life. The dichotomy between acquisition and the higher things of life is thereby dissolved, as Franklin understood Locke. That is why by the use of intelligence and reason one does not pursue present-oriented satisfactions and pleasures but becomes future oriented. One invests in the more rewarding pleasures of the future. This is the mentality of the capitalist, of the entrepreneur, of the investor. And this is identified with civilizing behavior. It is the poor yokel, the illiterate, who by virtue of his lack of breeding, of upbringing, is condemned to the feeble use of the faculty that nature gave him—reason—and therefore remains poor, which is deplorable. This of course is intimately tied with the idea of human freedom, liberty. Hence, as one is more reasonable, one attains freedom—which is the really important payoff of the use of these God-given faculties.

MR. GOLDWIN: How do you answer this question of the extent to which commerce is the spirit of the Constitution?

MR. BANFIELD: The distinction seems rather artificially made between the society being acquisitive or commercial on the one hand and higher things existing on the other. For Locke acquisitiveness was a necessary condition of aspiration toward higher things. Now just what the higher things are depends largely on the capacities and tastes of the individual. Some people would perhaps pursue the individual exercises of rational choice, and others would not. For Franklin, and possibly for others who more or less consciously followed this line of thought, the distinction between acquisitiveness on the one hand and pursuit of the higher things on the other was nonexistent.

3
Democracy

ROBERT GOLDWIN: When someone complains that some aspect of American politics is not democratic, there is a common quip that we are not after all a democracy but a republic. And what is meant by this quip of course is that many provisions of the constitutional system are not strictly in accord with majority rule. That is clearly seen in all the fractions in the Constitution. An amendment, for instance, must be proposed by two-thirds of both houses of Congress and ratified by three-fourths of the states. In the ratification of treaties, one-third of the Senate can defeat even a very popular treaty.

The electoral college is another institution that is not run strictly according to majority rule. It is possible for a candidate who has the popular majority of votes to lose an election. We see it in the Senate, which is not apportioned by population. The Senate can approve legislation by the vote of a majority of senators who represent a small proportion of the population of the nation. And of course the Supreme Court is not elected at all.

These provisions of the Constitution have been called obstacles to democratic rule by knowledgeable commentators on the Constitution. Yet it seems clear to many that ours is a system of popular government, that public opinion does rule, and that what the people—or a majority of them—want, the people get, ultimately at least, if not immediately.

Having posed the most obvious difficulty of speaking of the Constitution as democratic, or as undemocratic, let me pose the same question that I have posed in previous sessions. To what extent, and in what ways, can it be said that democracy is the spirit of the Constitution?

TERENCE MARSHALL: The issue is what Madison might mean when he refers to the United States as a representative democracy. Obviously the qualification that he gives to democracy has been a source of criticism: in some ways democracy itself becomes attenuated to a point that it no longer is democratic. That raises the issue of the relationship between democracy and good government.

If one looks at the problem of democracy as the founders saw it, there were three themes: majority rule, equality of rights, and competence.

The framers said that a popular government can be unstable or incompetent as well as unjust, and they sought solutions to it. Those solutions of course are well known in the various institutions of the United States: federalism, separation of powers, and commerce.

When one looks at *Federalist* No. 10, for example, it seems that critics have emphasized commerce in abstraction from other considerations there. Madison in that work was concerned with what one could call the three elements of the soul, namely, reason, passion, and interest. Madison noted that passions and interests dominate in politics, and at the same time he wished to find some place in this domain for reasonableness. His famous solution is the multiplication of factions, or interest groups, so that they can form majorities only factitiously, or artificially, so that there can be no dominant class or mass movement based on interest or passion. This leads to the argument for the commercial republic, and therefore the capitalist society, which would encourage fragmentation.

The solution to the problem of democratic government that Madison and the principal founders sought, is to establish what they called inventions of prudence, devices such as the commercial republic and separation of powers, that might channel the interests and the passions of the people in a way that gives some place for reasonableness in a democratic society.

The effect of the commercial republic is to attenuate the passions and the interests in a way that differs from the classical attempt to refine the passions and interests by education. That solution proposed by Madison for the attenuation of passions and interests is more consistent with the qualities of the ordinary human being and therefore is more consistent with democracy.

Finally, one notices that a particular human quality becomes inscribed in the Constitution by virtue of these institutional devices, namely, a certain moderation of the passions, a moderation that is itself a precondition, on the highest level, of prudential judgment and therefore of the capacity for deliberation. Moderation is itself, again, a democratic virtue, a popular virtue, rather than an aristocratic virtue. There is no formal cultivation of the highest form of prudence under this constitutional design, but when one looks at the federal devices, one might say that the federal structure of the regime might have provided the conditions for the formation of character that, on the national level at least, could become refined to judge the questions of practice from this level of prudence.

In that sense the United States is a popular regime. It is a regime in which the ordinary qualities are relied upon—ordinary qualities that might be interested or ambitious or, in a higher form, moderate. At the same time the United States is a constitutional democracy precisely because the Constitution restrains these passions in a way that is consistent with democracy.

BENJAMIN BARBER: The letter of the American Constitution is at best distrustful of democracy, for the most part undemocratic, and in certain instances antidemocratic. But the "spirit" or "ethos," as the word has been used here, of the Constitution can be and historically has been employed in the name of democracy. It is the spirit, fortunately, that has counted for the most part in the history of the republic.

The letter of the Constitution—and Robert Goldwin suggested a number of the obvious devices—is one of distrust of democracy. The representative principle is an effort to filter popular opinion rather than to embody it. Even some of the more democratic proponents of the founding were distrustful of democracy. Jefferson had aristocratic as well as democratic propensities. On the whole this meant that in the era of the Constitution the Antifederalists, to the extent they were democrats, found themselves viewing the Constitution as a threat to democracy as democracy had been embodied, say, in the Pennsylvania Constitution or in the rights of local citizenry to direct participation on the one-man, one-vote principle. Such principles were seen by the Antifederalists as principles that the Constitution not only did not attempt to embody but in fact assailed.

One hundred years later, the Progressives also came to see the Constitution as an essentially antidemocratic instrument of hegemonic class interests. To the extent the letter of the Constitution has prevailed, it may appear that the struggle for democracy in America has been a struggle against the Constitution. The struggle for democracy that has failed has taken the Constitution as its adversary because the Constitution has been too narrowly construed.

The successful path of democracy in America has always ignored or overlooked the letter of the Constitution in favor of its spirit, its rhetoric, and its ethos. On this path we talk not so much about the Constitution as a document but as a body of documents including the state constitutions and the Declaration of Independence and about the political practices that arose out of the application of the Constitution to the real political issues of the time.

I think particularly of the rhetoric of the Declaration as the rhetoric of the constitutional heritage: "all men are created equal," "we, the people." Patrick Henry said that "we, the people" had never been authorized by the people. Nonetheless the people utilized the phrase in subsequent decades to struggle to make the principle true. There is also the rights talk of the Bill of Rights, and of the state constitutions, as well as the civic republican talk that was a background for the Constitution. All of these became central to the struggle for extended suffrage, the struggle to democratize the Constitution.

This strategy has been relatively successful. Universal suffrage, protection of rights, and political equality have been won by defining the constitutional heritage in terms of its ethos and spirit, rather than in terms of its letter. But when we consider economic and social equality, or social justice, the letter of the Constitution, not its spirit, has prevailed.

There is a good deal of room for criticism of the letter of the Constitution, but that criticism has been successful, and can be successful, only when it embraces the ethos, the spirit, and the rhetoric of the constitutional heritage and uses those to reform the actual document to extend and enlarge it in democratic directions.

ABNER MIKVA: Professor Barber has suggested that the efforts to paint the Constitution as an obstacle to democratization have failed. When we talk about how democratic the spirit of the Constitution is, I want to know the context. Nobody really wants the idea of total democracy to cover all the institutions of government. I picture the democratic court system, the democratic criminal justice system, where we put every defendant to a popular vote to decide guilt or innocence. No one would call that a justice system. At least we did not when France was trying it after its revolution.

Nor does the Congress run altogether as a democratic system. The idea of all 435 prima donnas in that body—in which I served— functioning without any rules, all of which are antidemocratic in their function, and in their design and in their purpose, boggles the mind.

So the real question is, What is meant by democracy? What is meant by "a spirit of democracy"? Our founding fathers—and using that term in itself suggests part of the problem—really did have a concern about universal suffrage. It really worried them. They worried in all kinds of ways. They obviously worried about blacks voting, about Indians voting. It never even occurred to them to worry about women voting, but they would have worried about it if somebody had suggested it. They worried about nonproperty owners voting. The original difficulties that the Constitution provided—for which it has taken us five amendments of the twenty-six that have been ratified— have to do with suffrage.

We needed an amendment to revoke their grand solution for blacks. We needed an amendment to guarantee women suffrage. We needed an amendment to change the age of suffrage. We needed an amendment to change the property requirement—although that did not really do much. The poll tax by that time had almost been abolished, but at least it did take an amendment.

In all these instances the efforts on the part of the electorate acting through the Congress, and acting through the amendment ratification process, to change the Constitution, were successful in eliminating some of the unnecessary obstacles that the founders put in place. But a few problems are still left. I continue to worry about the electoral college, for example. If we were to make an institutional change, that would be the one place where I would like to see it. Actually we could do so without a constitutional amendment. We probably could do it simply by changing the way we apportion the electoral vote. But a continuing worry is that we still have a system where losers can be winners; this has happened several times in our history. According to some figures it happened as recently as 1960, when someone with fewer popular votes defeated somebody with more popular votes. That is a troublesome notion by any definition of democracy. But beyond suffrage, the spirit of the Constitution has in fact been both democratic in its origin and democratic in its application.

CHARLES KRAUTHAMMER: Picking up on Judge Mikva's point, I suggest that Professor Barber's implicit point—that democratization is always inherently good—ought to be questioned. If we define democracy as Madison did, as popular control of government, the more immediate that control, the more democratic the system. It seems obvious that there must be a balance, and that any system that is exclusively or to an extreme extent democratic would be undesirable.

We now have the means, for example, for an instant polling of the population on any issue. Direct democracy was possible for the ancients only in small republics. It is now possible in a continental country like ours, but it would obviously be rejected, out of hand, as totally inimical to good government.

So the question is not how democratic a system ought to be— with the assumption that the more democracy the better. The question is what ought to be the balance between democratic control of government and, as Professor Barber would call them, nondemocratic or antidemocratic strengths, which were built in rather obsessively by the founders. One contemporary example is the choosing of a presidential candidate by the Democratic party. No one can deny that the process is infinitely more democratic in the sense of popular control than thirty years ago, but hardly anyone would argue that the product of that system is superior today than it was thirty or fifty years ago, when the men in the back room chose Franklin Roosevelt.

It is worth questioning the assumption that democratization is always inherently good. Clearly, when it means expanding the franchise, nobody would question that. But there is the real question of how much of a filter to put between popular will and Government action—not an assumption that popular will ought always prevail. Robert Goldwin said that in our system ultimately the people prevail. That is right. It ought to be ultimately and not immediately. And how immediate as opposed to ultimate is the question, and that is a question of balance.

EDWIN YODER: I would like to reinforce what Charles Krauthammer has said and to challenge Judge Mikva on the subject of the electoral college. The problem with the electoral college is that it is not functioning as was intended. Let me be quite reactionary about the way the presidential electoral system is working today. When the framers, at the Constitutional Convention, came to the question of the method of choosing a president, they sifted carefully through the alternatives, including direct popular election and election by the national legislature, which was contemplated in the Virginia plan; they settled upon the electoral college, which of course is not so named in the Constitution.

It seems intrinsically a vastly superior system to the system we are using today. In the system the framers contemplated, each state would in its own fashion—probably by the state legislature—select a body of notables equal in number to the representation in Congress. Each of those people—the electors—would then vote for two persons; the person with the greatest number of votes would be the president, and the runner-up would be vice president. The system was changed by the Twelfth Amendment.

But that point of delegating power has become increasingly apparent as we see the pyramid inverted in our present system of selection, whereby a few so-called political activists in a few states of debatable representativeness present us in effect with a fait accompli every four years. Certainly that seems to be true in the matter of the Democratic nomination. It can be argued that whereas the electoral college system as originally envisaged was a pyramid resting on its base, we now have inverted the pyramid to rest upon its apex. It has become increasingly less representative and certainly less successful in winnowing the possible candidates for president and therefore democratic in the root sense of the term—and not more democratic.

Many of the post-1968 reforms in the structure of the Democratic party have led to peculiar outcomes in the structuring of the Democratic convention (which are not immediately to the point since the Democratic convention has ceased to be a deliberative body making a decision about the nominee). We are presented at an increasingly early point, with a fait accompli in which there has been very little mass participation.

MR. MIKVA: I want to make sure about what we disagree. We could spend five days talking about what is wrong with the present system, starting with the primaries, the selection process of candidates. My question is, How would you propose that we elect a president of the United States? We agree that you do not like the present system.

MR. YODER: I would be happy to have a president elected by electors chosen in the states.

MR. MIKVA: Chosen by whom?

MR. YODER: By a democratic process to be determined by the states, as was envisaged in the Constitution.

MR. MIKVA: If the legislature seeks to choose or to name electors, that would be all right?

MR. YODER: Precisely so.

MR. MIKVA: And the electors would meet some place?

MR. YODER: They were supposed to meet in the states. The whole point was to avoid an agglomeration of the electors from which government by cabal of some sort could result. The decisions were to be made at the state level and forwarded, sealed, to Washington and there examined in the Senate.

MR. MIKVA: Presumably the electors could be chosen either in a popular election or by the state legislatures as the state might ordain. They would meet in their state. They would choose a candidate. Let us assume that we somehow figure out a marvelous primary system.

MR. YODER: They would make two choices.

MR. MIKVA: Would these electors be chosen for each party, or would there be just one group of electors?

MR. YODER: As the states might decide.

MR. MIKVA: So the state might say that we have thirty electoral votes coming, here are thirty electors, they can decide whomever they want.

MR. YODER: Precisely.

MR. MIKVA: There would be no popular input into their decision?

MR. YODER: The point—and it was the framers' assumption—is that the voting public in the states—to be sure, a much narrower public at that time than it is today—would take the most intense interest in how the electors were chosen, who were chosen as electors, and whom the electors then chose.

MR. MIKVA: The spirit of that is not only undemocratic. The consequences of it would be to remove the legitimacy of the president acting on behalf of all the people, which is the spirit of democracy.

EDWARD BANFIELD: I would like to move the discussion closer to Robert Goldwin's question. I offer a footnote to your initial remarks, Judge Mikva. It seems that the founders were undecided in their conception of who should rule or perhaps they were of two minds. They thought that there is such a thing as the common good or as they sometimes said, the "public happiness," as distinguished from happiness, as in "life, liberty and the pursuit of happiness." The notion of a common good as opposed to personal or private good was real. This was a heritage of Calvinism and the notion of a covenant with the people; it was strong in their mind. The task of the individual voter was to assume the role of citizen, as was the task of the states-man, and to perceive the common good.

This required a kind of disinterestedness and an ability to see political matters as a whole and, having seen them, to draw correct inferences for action. It was assumed that those who looked in this way—disinterestedly and reasonably, in the role of citizen—at the common interest would come to the same conclusion. But at the same time they thought that men were by nature self-interested, even rapacious, that with rare exceptions they would subordinate the pub-lic interest, if they had any conception of it, to their private or parochial advantage.

Both these conceptions prevailed, and so it seems that were were two spirits. In *The Federalist Papers* there are six references to hap-piness, and they all refer to the public happiness as opposed to the happiness of individuals. That two-mindedness is inherent in the nature of the whole matter, and it still prevails. It is a problem that is unresolved. Do we think of the voter acting in the role of citizen or acting in the role of interested party? One might think of abortion, for example, as bad from a public standpoint but good from a private standpoint. Which view is the relevant one? Judge Mikva remarked on the chaos that would result if in criminal procedures a democracy decided on the basis presumably of personal tastes whether to convict or release the accused. J. S. Mill says that the voter has no more right to take his personal views into account than the juror. It is a purely public question. Therefore voting should be open, with no privacy. When John Kennedy ran for president, the Catholic archbishop of Milwaukee announced that a Catholic voting for Kennedy because he was a Catholic, was committing a sin. I do not remember whether it was a mortal sin or a venial sin, but it was a sin, and that struck me as anomalous. Because if the Catholic thought that here is a man who adheres to certain principles of virtue and right living and behavior and public conduct—that the voter adheres to—why should it be a sin to vote for him?

Is it a sin for farmers to vote for a candidate who they think is going to raise farm prices? Is it a sin for black people to vote for candidates because they are black? Reverend Jesse Jackson would not agree with the archbishop of Milwaukee. He certainly does not think that whites ought to vote for whites because they are white. But it is a problem. The system could not possibly work as we want it to work if nobody voted for his interests. It is essential somehow to know, to get a tabulation, of who feels he has benefited.

We want to take both into account: private happiness, as well as the public happiness. How do we do it through a voting process?

There are some interesting empirical studies on voting behavior, or attitude surveys, that have been done in recent years. Apparently people do vote differently depending on whether they think of themselves as voting for their own interest or for the public interest as they perceive it.

MR. MARSHALL: I would add a comment concerning the discussion on the electoral college, to link that with the subject of democracy. It may be useful to relate that to the problem of majority rule as opposed to constitutional democracy and at the same time to recall that, because of the districting system, many times in this century the congressional majority has not been the same as the national electoral majority. And of course there is not really a debate in the United States to eliminate the districting system. We have a national congressional majority that does not correspond exactly with the national electoral majority.

It is therefore useful to examine why, for the sake of equality, we would not wish to eliminate the districting system. A similar principle might apply to the defense of the electoral college. There is some relationship between that defense and federalism, for example; there is a relationship between the federal structure and the overall constitutional aim or the spirit of the Constitution. In that sense one might say that the problem of the electoral college can be linked with the problem of unrestrained majority rule as opposed to the problem of constitutional government.

MR. KRAUTHAMMER: The battle for the electoral college is lost. Direct popular elections of presidents, in effect, is the current system. It is slightly rigged in the sense that winning individual states counts for a certain number of points. Essentially the popular notion that a president ought to be elected popularly is already accepted, and it seems a good notion because of the legitimacy with which it imbues a president. South Korea has accepted that same principle; it is hardly one that we would want to go back on.

But to get back to the earlier point, no one would want Congress being more reflective of the aggregate vote of the people in congressional elections because that would sacrifice the districting system. The experience of countries with proportional representation without districts, like Israel—which is a quasi-anarchy—is an effective warning against systems without that filter. The districting system is a filter; it exaggerates majorities. In Britain it produced a huge majority for Margaret Thatcher, who won a landslide with 42 percent of the vote—and that is the way it should be. It produces what Hamilton would applaud as energetic government. It is a distortion of democracy, but in fact we cannot have pure democracy and function.

MR. YODER: There is an unstated and undemonstrated premise on the part of Judge Mikva and others that the present system is more representative of the democratic spirit of the country in any given presidential election than would be a literal application of the electoral college. I am a realist; we will not return to the system that had become essentially passé by the early 1800s. But if we could return and make a literal application of the electoral college system, we might come closer to the substance of representative democracy than we have in the essentially plebiscitary system that now operates, in which a handful of political activists, augmented and amplified by a handful of bellwether members of the press, in effect determine the presidential nominees.

MR. MIKVA: Those are not my views. I merely said that it might well be a better system. The problem it would cause would be the loss of legitimacy, and that would be awful to contemplate. If people knew about the electoral college, their reaction would be awful to contemplate. Fortunately, most of them do not know about it; they think that when they vote for Franklin D. Roosevelt, that is who they are voting for and that their vote is what counts. And if we ever went to a system that denigrated the importance of that vote, that would be bad for the spirit of the country, whether that is democratic or not.

MR. GOLDWIN: As I understand your argument, you mean that if a candidate for president did not get a plurality of the popular vote but did get a majority of the electoral vote, as happened in 1888, that would be considered illegitimate. What you mean is that people think that the only legitimate claim to the presidency comes from getting a plurality of the popular vote. And they do not get legitimacy from the constitutional majority, which is the electoral college. That is consistent with Professor Barber's argument that there is something that could be called the spirit of the Constitution but is not derived from the text of the Constitution and is separate and even opposed to the letter of the Constitution. I had always thought of the spirit of the Constitution as something that is derived from the Constitution itself, but you are finding a spirit that is somehow independent of the Constitution, and in essential ways opposed to it.

MR. MIKVA: In essential ways it is not opposed to it. Because of people's perception of the Constitution and government they think—rightly so, in most instances—that the system they have comes from the Constitution. Some of it comes by statute. But if you ask a person how our system was founded, the average voter would say that it comes through and under the Constitution; yet some things that people think they have under that Constitution are not there. One is that they think they directly elect the president. When people are asked how we elect our president, the overwhelming majority believe that whoever gets the most votes wins. That is what they think. It is like the right to privacy. People think that it is in the Constitution.

MR. GOLDWIN: Isn't there a duty, then, on the part of the people who know what the constitutional provision is, to insist that legitimacy comes from that? If they think that the Constitution ought to be amended, they still should abide by it until it is amended.

MR. MIKVA: First of all, we are abiding by the electoral college. Mr. Yoder is saying that it has not come down the way the people originally intended, but there is nothing unconstitutional about the way we elect our president. I do favor an amendment or at least a change in the system that would comport more with what people think is happening, than what could happen.

I would be troubled if we ever had a situation where someone with a substantial deficit in the popular vote became president of the United States. I say "deficit" to mean less votes than somebody else. That would provoke a serious crisis. This would be a constitutionally elected president, but the people would be unhappy about it and would resent the system that perpetrated what they would consider a fraud.

MR. BARBER: Let me respond to this question of the tension between the letter of the Constitution and its spirit. It is a logical, an intellectual contradiction. It is a happy event that the contradiction is there in American history. Revolution is the alternative to seeing a larger tradition that perhaps emanates from but may be in tension with the letter of the Constitution. That is to say, the alternative for democrats is to say our Constitution is undemocratic. That would leave democrats with revolution as their only option; there are progressives and others, some Marxists, who assume that position.

This position presents real dangers to the stability of America. Fortunately it is a tradition that has not been successful. The success of the system has come precisely because Americans have creatively misread their Constitution as being a good deal more democratic in spirit than it probably was, or than some of its current interpreters like Mr. Yoder would like it to be. Plenty of people today also distrust democracy in exactly the same way that many of the founders distrusted democracy.

But to suggest that we have an intellectual duty to point out to the American people that the Constitution does not license democracy—and if that is what they want, they had better look elsewhere—suggests that they ought to look to revolution. That is not a message anyone would want to hand to people looking for greater social justice, more suffrage, more democracy in the American system.

Mr. YODER: This is patently untenable. Judge Mikva certainly would not tolerate for a moment in the U.S. Court of Appeals a contention that simply because a majority of the American people have the illusion that federal juries function in such and such a way, or that jury trial requires less than unanimous verdicts in certain circumstances, this ought to overrule the letter and spirit of the Constitution in the sense in which Robert Goldwin is using the term and in which I would use the term.

If it is not a legitimate and demonstrable emanation from the letter of the Constitution, we get into deep water when we suggest this notion of creative constitutionalism. What are the boundaries of this creative constitutionalism?

Mr. MIKVA: Part of the problem comes from the fact that we are talking about the spirit of the Constitution. I find it much easier to talk about the spirit of the Declaration of Independence than I do about the spirit of the Constitution because unlike the Declaration of Independence, the Constitution is a set of orders, of rules, of specifics that tell us what to do.

In response to your question, of course I agree with you. The electoral college, as we now tolerate it and use it, is perfectly constitutional. You would not find anybody in the country who would say it is not. The concern with it is that it engenders this practical problem that some day might blow us up, and I worry about that. But you are absolutely right. The difficulty about talking about the Constitution and the spirit is that people have some kinds of feelings about their government that do not stem directly, word for word, from the Constitution—such as the thought that they directly elect their president.

That is not the way the Constitution works, but what we have is a constitutional system. It is close enough to what people think they ought to have that we can abide it. Some of us would like to see the system move closer to the expectation by changing that section of the

Constitution, just as we did the age of voters, the election of senators, and so on.

MR. GOLDWIN: I remember an essay by Professor Banfield in which he explained how a few modifications away from pure democratic process produce more democratic results than strict adherence to democratic procedures. I hope that this discussion will not completely omit that explanation, or some part of it.

MR. BANFIELD: To try to recall the essay would be unfair to it. But the gist of it was that in the reform of the party system, by getting rid of the smoke-filled rooms and in general achieving more democratic procedures, we have rendered the party system unworkable, or at least less successfully workable than it was before we began to tamper with it. This is particularly the case with the reforms made in the Democratic party, but the Republican party has gone much the same way.

MR. GOLDWIN: The application to our present discussion would be this. That certain provisions of the Constitution do not seem in accord with the principle of majority rule is not sufficient evidence that the spirit and intention of the Constitution are undemocratic. And when Madison spoke about auxiliary provisions, the proper understanding of them was as devices not to thwart popular government but to make it effective.

MR. KRAUTHAMMER: You cannot have it both ways. If you want to argue that certain, less democratic provisions—smoke-filled rooms, electoral colleges, districting—are useful and produce good government, that is one argument. And that is the argument of the founders. That is what *The Federalist* is all about. It is a relentless attack on pure democracy in the name of good government and the common good. But you cannot argue that less democracy makes for more democracy.

You have to choose your values. Sometimes you sacrifice democracy to achieve other goods, such as the common good as the founders would have called it or the public interest as we would. The founders did not argue that with judicial review or the veto power they were being more democratic. They were arguing that they were being more constitutional and producing better government.

MR. GOLDWIN: In one respect it is important to disagree with you: they started with the historical evidence that all previous popular governments had failed. The question was how to devise a popular government that would thrive. They did not see these provisions as an opposition of democracy versus effective government but as necessary devices to make democratic government effective so that it would survive. Therefore those supposedly undemocratic provisions were in the service of democracy.

MR. KRAUTHAMMER: But they were not arguing that by putting restraints on popular control, they were actually augmenting democracy. They were saying that to preserve it, they must diminish it. That seems to be a reasonable argument.

MR. BANFIELD: In common, ordinary language we sometimes use the word "democratic" to describe a country where people's rights are respected. My point in the piece that Robert Goldwin mentioned was that there is a tension but not a downright antagonism between democracy of procedure—one man, one vote—and democracy of results—preservation of individual rights. I am not saying anything really different from what you are, except incorporating the word "democracy" in both senses, which is perhaps adding to the confusion.

MR. YODER: I agree with Robert Goldwin's reservations about Charles Krauthammer's point. Here is the essential point. Most of the framers would have said that the fundamental credo of our political system is stated in the Declaration of Independence: governments are instituted among men and derive their just powers from the consent of the governed. It does not say from the agreement of the governed. It says from the consent of the governed. They would not have been troubled by our modern sense that democracy must be defined as a form of populistic mainlining of transitory whims into public policy. That is the definition of democracy that probably 85 or 90 percent of the American people would use today. But, the framers would not have shared that view. They saw democracy as, in essence, government by consent.

MR. KRAUTHAMMER: Madison's definition of democracy in *The Federalist* is exactly that, the Athenian model of popular control, and he was against it.

JOSEPH CROPSEY: Among the many things that the Constitution does not mention by name, democracy is one. I have never heard it maintained that this was in the strict sense a democracy. I have often heard it said that this was something like what the ancient people and others more recently called a mixed regime. That there are elements of democracy is the presupposition of your question, which is to say, To what extent is the Constitution democratic, implying to what extent is it not democratic.

To begin to look at the question, without some quantitative intention in mind, we can ask ourselves what would be a wholly democratic regime. A wholly democratic regime is inconceivable under modern circumstances. It was defined in antiquity for all time. It is a regime in which all of the people directly participate, without representation, directly in assemblies, coming together and voting on all issues. There was another qualification, namely, that all the partici-pants, that is to say, all the citizens, however they may define them-selves—this by the way is compatible with a society with slaves, in which people could simply define out a large number of human beings—should be eligible for office. The honors and perquisites and benefits of public life should be available to every citizen, and every citizen should be present, as far as possible, in an assembly in which the issues of the time are disposed of.

The question is therefore, What institutions were available, which were written into both the letter and the spirit of the United States Constitution and were not simply democratic? Now if, as Judge Mikva made plain, there is a sense on the part of the people that some outcome is not strictly democratic and is therefore illegitimate, then one would not say that something has emerged that belongs to the spirit of the Constitution—which is different from the letter. Rather something has come over the opinion of the public and has moved it in a direction that is different from both the spirit and the letter of the Constitution.

If there is a significant disjunction between the spirit and the letter of the Constitution, my first inclination would be to conclude that the founders were in some sense confused, that they did not incarnate the spirit in the letter with sufficient success or clarity. As our history evolved, one might see the two of them as divergent. That might in fact be the case. I am not enough of a constitutional scholar to know that. But if we begin with the premise that there is a dif-ference between spirit and letter, we have to accept the accompanying proposition that there was confusion at the inscription of the letter. I would rather suppose that something has entered our public life from outside the Constitution and has created a climate of opinion that differs significantly from both the spirit and the letter of the Constitu-tion in favor of a notion of democracy that itself may be somehow unsatisfactory.

MR. BARBER: I would rather say that there was conflict, not con-fusion. There was conflict, and the Constitution represents one phase in a long process that includes the Declaratin of Independence, the Articles, state constitutions, the era of the Bill of Rights, right down to the Civil War. The larger spirit—and I agree with Judge Mikva that perhaps we should not speak of the spirit of the Constitution but of the spirit of the founding, or the spirit of America, or the spirit of the American constitutional republic—arises out of those conflicts.

But simply to choose the Constitution as the particular victory of one set of compromises among those who were in conflict with one another, and then to suggest that it defines America, and nothing else can, or to suggest that if there is a tension, it is the result of confusion—this is too narrow a definition of America. The larger definition has been guiding actual American politics. That is one of the clues to the success of the politics of America. The larger tradition includes the Constitution but is not limited to and cannot be interpreted in an exclusively antidemocratic fashion. Most people on the panel, whether they are for or against democracy, have agreed that this larger tradition prevailed.

MR. KRAUTHAMMER: Let me make one point about Professor Barber's framing of the question. He began by saying that the spirit of the Constitution was democratic, and now I detect some shifting of his position where he concedes that perhaps it is not the spirit of the document but the spirit of America. The spirit of America is a far more nebulous and malleable notion than the spirit of the Constitution. If you study the Constitution and you study those who wrote about it, it is hard to argue that they had this notion of democracy that Professor Barber attributes to the spirit of America.

The Federalist seems to put a fence around the House of Representatives, which is the most democratic body in the structure of the government. It is clear that the founders saw democracy as instrumental, and not as an end in itself. That is the fundamental difference between what Professor Barber is calling the spirit of America, which I would say is the spirit of contemporary America, which does see democracy as an end in itself, rather than an instrument, and what the founders considered the spirit of their constitution.

The founders conceived of democracy instrumentally because their notion of the end of government was what they called good government or the happiness of the people or notions that we now look at as rather quaint. Some people have substituted democracy as an end in itself. Others have substituted equality or liberty, depending on their ideological predisposition. But to argue that the spirit of the Constitution is one that coincides with our notion of democracy as an end in itself, is simply historically false.

MR. BARBER: I would not argue that the Constitution is either democratic or anti-democratic. That is certainly not the definition. Here Professor Banfield's definition, which he adduced early in our discussion but to which we did not really refer, is important: the notion of public good, with the citizen as someone who tends to the public good. The letter of the Constitution itself is devoted to the notion of good government, government by citizens who attend to the public good. The question is who should count as citizens. The

Constitution makes them a narrow caste of specially chosen and specially insulated governors. It is the aim of the ancient democrat to make them the whole citizen body.

The modern democratic citizen, voting his own special interests, represents neither of those two notions of democracy: neither the notion of the aristocratic governor insulated by the filters of representation from the people nor ancient citizen bodies governing themselves together in deliberative assemblies. One problem, the misstep in the Constitution, is that in its letter it tries to insulate citizens from the mass of the people by creating a kind of professional caste of aristocratic governors, instead of trying to find ways of empowering the larger citizenry in ways that made them deliberative, public-spirited citizens. This "misstep" contributed to the modern notion of the citizen as a privatized, self-interested client of government and in that sense contributed to the problems of elite versus mass democracy that we experience today.

MR. KRAUTHAMMER: Madison had a far less sanguine notion of the virtue and the disinterestedness of what you call the aristocratic class of governors than you portray. He clearly, in setting up this remarkably complicated system of checks, was trying to restrain the passions of this class of governors because he trusted their passions not much more than he trusted the passions of the citizen. I am not sure that he had this notion of a disinterested class. He saw them as susceptible to the power and passion and self-interest as the mass of citizens and tried to create a structure that would constrain that passion.

MR. MARSHALL: Madison, at the end of his life, wrote a letter, which apparently was not sent, about majority governments. In that letter he refers to majority governments as the least bad of practicable regimes. When we link that with his argument in *Federalist* No. 49, it is useful to bear in mind his criticism of Jefferson's proposal for referenda: the United States is not composed of a nation of philosophers, not composed even of people who love wisdom as opposed to people who might be wise. That remark parallels what he says in *Federalist* No. 10 about the absence of statesmen. If we link these themes about the problem of the least bad regime, we might say that the Constitution takes the common man, as he ordinarily is with his defects as well as the qualities he might possess, and seeks to constitute a decent popular regime, with a view to which qualities are normally lacking as well as to which are possible among ordinary people.

JAMES CEASER: I agree completely with Charles Krauthammer's formulation that this was not pure democracy. But it is important not to make the founding appear more undemocratic than it was. There is a powerful element of democracy in the founding. To see the spirit of democracy, as we know it today, as developing wholly in opposition to the Constitution is an incorrect reading of the historical evidence. Therefore it is important not to look at the founding through the eyes of certain historians who wanted to depict it in a most undemocratic fashion. Look, for example, at the way the House of Representatives was chosen.

Suffrage for the House of Representatives was the same as for the popular bodies in the states, and yet everyone seems to agree that the states at the time were fairly popular instruments; you yourself, Professor Barber, in speaking of the alternate sources of the spirit, refer to the state constitution. So the founders were no less democratic than the state constitutions in regard to suffrage.

In addition, the development of mass democracy, aside from the problem of slaves and women, occurred in the United States before it did in any other country in the world and without any constitutional amendment. Therefore the development of a large, modern suffrage was wholly consistent with our Constitution and did not require amendment.

For the election of the president, the record of the electoral college system shows that the original is not the same as the system we have today; there are many differences, for many historical reasons. Nonetheless, the convention record shows that the electoral system was probably the most popular system practicable at that time to choose the president. And its spirit was in many senses of the word truly democratic. If we could discuss the question at some other point, the Constitution of the founding, as it was first implemented, is far more democratic in certain respects than the Constitution we have today, given the role of the bureaucracy and the courts.

MR. MIKVA: Until this last half minute I was nodding my head vigorously in assent because by concentrating on just the suffrage part we looked at what was the most undemocratic part of the Constitution. But many of the other institutions of government that were proclaimed by the Constitution, including the Congress, are far more democratic than any institutions that were known at the time, better than and certainly no worse than the state legislatures, and much more democratic in the way they functioned. Bicameralism was in fact a democratic notion rather than an antidemocratic one.

There was some tension about suffrage. There were people who were proposing the direct election of the president, and they were overwhelmingly defeated by people who offered speeches that would cause them to be run out of town today. But in looking at suffrage—not the electoral college alone—we have been focusing on that part of the Constitution that compared to our present notions of democracy least resembles what we have today. Congress still functions much the way it did in 1789. Some people complain about that. I think it is good.

MR. GOLDWIN: On the matter of suffrage, Judge Mikva, you have made the point many times that the Constitution is more generous on the question of women voting than any of the state constitutions or the Northwest Ordinance.

MR. MIKVA: And they were more generous on property; there were no property qualifications. But it took five amendments to get us where we are today with suffrage.

HARVEY FLAUMENHAFT: The problem now is that democracy is the good word, and in a way it obscures the issue. There is no doubt that the framers were committed to popular government, and popular government meant representative government for them because a government that is not representative means, for instance, the vast body of the people doing all kinds of things, that means that they are poor and their lives are nastier. An assembly of the armed people: that is the classical polis. At one point in *The Federalist* it is even said that if the people do nothing but choose every official, they would have no time for anything else.

So, there is a commitment, precisely on popular grounds, to representative government, and once you have representative government, the question is, What will make it work? What will make it last? It is not clear that having the representatives immediately responsible to a vote of the entire populace brings about the desired result, as has been pointed out several times.

The framers were concerned about popular outcomes that are popular in the long run, and thus—for precisely what we would call democratic reasons—procedures that would seem on their face to be less than democratic might be instituted. In one sense of the word, for instance, it might be more democratic for representatives to have longer terms simply because some things require a long time to show whether they work. And if every decision must be judged six months later, decisions that require more than six months to be judged will not be undertaken by government.

It is not clear whether this is a matter of the principle of popularity versus the principle of workability. There are also cases in which the popular principle itself requires that people who make the ultimate judgment keep hands off for a while simply because of the time required to judge the decision.

4
Liberty and Equality

ROBERT GOLDWIN: The Constitution is remarkably silent about principles, quite unlike other documents written at the same time. It is common, therefore, for many to assert, and others to deny, that principles like liberty and equality are embedded in the Constitution, although unmentioned. The disagreement often takes the form of a dispute about the relationship of the Declaration of Independence and the Constitution. In the best-known book on the Declaration of Independence, by Carl Becker, the argument is made, for example, that the Declaration was useful for the purposes of revolution but not useful for sustaining a constitutional government. Russell Kirk, the prominent conservative author, praised the conservative good sense of the Constitution because it turned away from the revolutionary folly of the Declaration of Independence. And Forrest McDonald, who gave the 1987 Jefferson Lecture in Washington, asserted as fact that from 1792 to 1861 no official American document spoke approvingly of the Declaration of Independence. The exception, in 1861, was South Carolina's declaration of secession from the Union.

On the other side Martin Diamond, in a memorable lecture given for the American Enterprise Institute on the occasion of the Bicentennial of the Declaration of Independence, made the argument that the two documents, the Constitution and the Declaration of Independence, are inseparable and that one cannot be understood independent of the other. This side of the argument is that the spirit of the Constitution is in fact the Declaration of Independence and that the structure of 1787 was designed above all to fulfill the principles of 1776. Foremost among those principles are the "truths," "self-evident truths," "that all men are created equal and that they are endowed . . . with certain unalienable rights," among which are "life, liberty, and the pursuit of happiness."

Others object that in critical respects the constitutional system compromised, contradicted, and even rejected the equal rights proclaimed by the Declaration. The institution of slavery, seemingly protected by the Constitution, raises serious questions about the connection of the Declaration and the Constitution.

And so I pose this question. To what extent, and in what ways, can it be said that liberty and equality are the spirit of the Constitution?

DICK HOWARD: As I listened to earlier panels, I was struck by the interrelation of words like "democracy," "liberty," "equality," and "federalism." Tocqueville in *Democracy in America* observed that several tendencies lend themselves to centralization of power in any democratic Western regime, of which America would be counted as one. He pointed in particular to the aspiration of democratic governments, or regimes, for what he called justice.

I suspect that in the sense Tocqueville was talking about justice, its nearest counterpart in our dialogue would be the word "equality," because Tocqueville argued, or at least he picked up on the argument he attributed to democrats, that if all human beings are in fact equal in the sense connoted in the Declaration of Independence, should they not be treated in the same way? That's the logical outgrowth of justice and equality. That would lead naturally to centralization precisely because a more centralized government is an efficient way of being sure that when people are before the law or are subject to government actions, they will in fact be treated in a standardized or uniform fashion.

As in so many things, Tocqueville was prescient in this. Much of the course of American history has been an effort to use federal power to achieve twin objectives: the dualism of liberty and equality, roughly but not perfectly approximated by due process and equal protection.

One of the things we might try to do in this session is see whether those constitutional phrases—"due process" and "equal protection"—are useful as surrogates for somewhat more theoretical ideas such as liberty and equality. Certainly the turning point in this respect is the adoption of the Fourteenth Amendment. After the adoption of the original Constitution and Bill of Rights, the most important single juridical event in American constitutional history is the adoption of that amendment because that amendment enhances both congressional power under section 5 and judicial power under section 1.

In relating this discussion to the previous consideration about federalism, I was intrigued that in an effort to define liberty, a panel suggested that there are at least two rather distinct definitions of liberty. One is the notion of simply being left alone. And that is the sense in which the due process clause has been used by the Court to expand zones of personal autonomy. But the other definition of liberty is essentially the right of choice, or self-government.

One of the questions raised in the discussion about federalism was whether the enhancement of federal power under the Fourteenth Amendment, while it may have enhanced equality and liberty in that sense of personal autonomy, may not have undermined and eroded liberty in the sense of the right of choice. While trying to strike some definition of liberty and equality and deciding to what extent they are part of the spirit of the Constitution, we should keep in our peripheral vision the way in which decisions on those questions have an impact on liberty in this other sense of right of choice.

WALTER BERNS: The statements attributed to Forrest McDonald and Carl Becker serve to depreciate the Declaration of Independence and its connection with the Constitution. After Article VII of the Constitution, the last article of the original, unamended Constitution, the Constitution reads "done in Convention, by the unanimous consent of the States present, the Seventeenth day of September in the year of our Lord one thousand seven hundred and eighty seven, and of the Independence of the United States of America the twelfth." In other words the United States began in 1776. Right in the Constitution itself the framers asserted a connection between the Declaration of Independence and the Constitution.

By itself of course that does not prove a dedication to the principles of the Declaration of Independence, but I would like to offer some evidence to demonstrate that connection. So intimate was the connection between the Declaration and the Constitution, that when the southern states pretended to secede from the Union and to form what they called the Confederate States of America, the vice president of the so-called Confederate States of America, Alexander Hamilton Stevens, made a speech in Savannah, Georgia, March 21, 1861, in which he said the following:

> The prevailing ideas entertained by [Jefferson] and most of the leading statesmen at the time of the formation of the old Constitution [which is to say our Constitution], were that the enslavement of the African was in violation of the laws of nature: that it was wrong in principle, socially, morally, and politically. It was an evil they knew not well how to deal with, but the general opinion of the men of that day was, that somehow or other, in the order of Providence, the institution would be evanescent and pass away. . . . Those ideas, however, were fundamentally wrong. They rested upon the assumption of the equality of races. This was an error. It was a sandy foundation, and the idea of a government built upon it; when the "storm came and the winds blew, it fell." Our

new government [that is, the new constitution of the Confederate States of America] is founded upon exactly the opposite idea; its foundations are laid, its cornerstone rests upon the great truth that the Negro is not equal to the white man. That slavery, subordination to the superior race, is his natural and normal condition. This, our new Government, is the first, in the history of the world based upon this great physical and moral truth.

That is the end of the statement; it is not the end of the speech. This man, speaking for the Confederate States of America, knew well that the principles of the Declaration of Independence were embodied in the Constitution of the United States, and it was precisely for that reason that these people pretended to secede from the Union and establish a new government.

WILLIAM ALLEN: This seems a good point at which to talk about the Declaration in light of the distinction that has been raised. I have often been curious as to why we tend to talk equally about liberty and equality as aspects of our political lives that are to be accomplished somehow through the work of government. In some respect the questions that Dick Howard brought out, suggest that.

In the Declaration we speak of securing these rights, meaning life, liberty, and the pursuit of happiness. We never speak in the Declaration of securing equality. Indeed the Declaration speaks of equality as created. Men are created equal. It seems to be a fact accomplished, not to be revisited, in the language of the Declaration. The tension that we hear so familiarly spoken of, between liberty and equality, may well be mistaken. The idea of equality as something that society produces through governmental institutions in fact undermines that posture in the Declaration of Independence, which says that society itself proceeds from equality and is not itself the producer of the equality of human beings.

That would force us to take much more seriously the question whether indeed the latter amendments to the Constitution, including the Fourteenth, can in some way have compromised that original perspective that is in the Declaration of Independence.

If men are created equal, and if from that equality government proceeds on the basis of the foundation of consent, then it follows equally well that we cannot translate the equality of the Declaration either into the terms of justice as they were used by Tocqueville, or into the terms more particularly used by McDonald in the Jefferson lecture. To say that the Declaration has not been cited officially, and to hold the Constitution or the community liable on that account, strikes me roughly equivalent to holding the Torah liable for not giving thematic discussions of the dimensions of piety and to assuming therefore that piety somehow was not important because in the Torah itself it is not laid out in programmatic fashion. The Northwest Ordinance of 1787, reconfirmed of course in the first Congress, uses terms of social compact compatible with that notion of equality in the Declaration of Independence and makes it clear that it is the foundation of the Constitution such that one cannot talk about the Constitution without first accepting the claims of the Declaration, namely, that all men are created equal.

CHARLES FAIRBANKS: The Constitution does try to have an effect upon equality in at least two clear ways. One of them is the attack on hereditary distinctions: the United States shall not give titles of nobility, the states shall not give titles of nobility, and no attainder of treason shall work corruption of blood, which is the same theme. Then the Constitution also defines the status of slavery as something that is permitted in practice but not legitimate because it is not talked about by its own name. The Constitution was trying to do something vis-à-vis equality.

PATRICIA WALD: When the founders came together in 1787, the major problem before the convocation was whether there would be an effective union in place of what had been too decentralized an association of states. And in that sense I look with some optimism upon some of the indicia in the main part of the Constitution itself, in terms of the protection of liberties versus this central government. There was an assumption that the states had been closer to the people and that the states were protective of the liberties of the people. Much later, well into the nineteenth century, the state became the villain.

The body of the document itself has some indicia of individual liberties—the ban on bills of attainder and the ex post facto laws, even the contract clause and the privileges and immunities clause suggest that they were thinking about liberty.

I also agree with Professor Fairbanks: with slavery they knew they were dealing with a terrible problem that they did not know how to solve, but that did not mean they should stop having a Constitution and a Union just because they could not solve it. And the fact that they put some limits on it such as the period for the importation of slaves, suggesting it would be regulable in the future, and even the three-fifths clause suggests that at least they were equivocal about it.

Finally, the fact that the Bill of Rights eventually became a big item and quickly was added to the Constitution; it gave a plethora of rights to the individual, secured against the federal government, not the states, because at that point the federal government looked like the prime threat to those individual liberties. All this suggests at least that they were thinking about these things. And I am not as dis-

couraged as some people are about the fact they did not solve the slavery problem within the Constitution. Had they tried, we might well not have had a Union.

HERMAN BELZ: My reaction to the problem of liberty and equality as part of the spirit of the Constitution is, first, if anything fulfills requirements of becoming part of the spirit of the Constitution, it would seem to be liberty and equality. That could lead to a discussion of whether the idea that the Constitution has a spirit is a problematic idea nowadays, whereas thirty, forty, fifty, one hundred years ago it was not at all problematic to talk about whether there is a spirit of the Constitution. That intrigues me as a political and intellectual problem of the last decade or more.

But, second, what is really problematic is the relationship between liberty and equality. Liberty is problematic because we still have the debate about what liberty in the Constitution is. Is it negative liberty, acquisitive liberty, or positive political liberty? Perhaps there is less dispute about equality, generally speaking, as historians and political scientists think about it, probably because they think that the Fourteenth Amendment introduces the idea of equality into the Constitution. The question about the Fourteenth Amendment is whether it is kind of a declaratory amendment or whether it really introduces a new element. It does not introduce a wholly new amendment. I think along the lines that Walter Berns does.

MR. ALLEN: I am not certain that there is less dispute about equality than about liberty in the colloquial view of the matter. It seems that while the Fourteenth Amendment may be reducible to the standard of the Declaration, the fifth clause of that amendment conveying to Congress the power to enforce the requirements of equal protection, may not mean the power to create equality.

It is clear that we have struggled ever since then over precisely the question of what kind of power this is and what kind of equality results. I am reminded of a lecture that Thomas Mann delivered in Claremont in 1941, on war and democracy. In this lecture—and this is the same Thomas Mann who had written earlier *Hitler, My Brother*—he went on to speak about liberty and equality or, in his language of that day, freedom and equality and a tension between them. The tension arose from the fact that equality was viewed as a constructive work of political society, something to be produced by policies and therefore to be imposed upon people, whereas freedom—whether to be left alone or otherwise defined—represented somehow primarily exemption from the constructive powers of government. Defined that way the tension is inevitable, and it seems that those kinds of tensions would have resulted from the Fourteenth Amendment.

I regard that as a misconstruction of the relationship of liberty and equality. There is no tension at all between them as they are formulated in the Declaration of Independence, but we have disputed, long and hot, over precisely the kind of tension that Mann described in that 1941 lecture.

MR. GOLDWIN: Why is there that tension between liberty and equality? Is it because the meaning of liberty has changed in our minds or because the meaning of equality has changed? If there was no tension, and there is now, something has changed.

MR. FAIRBANKS: Isn't it the gradual submergence of the understanding of liberty as self-government, which it seems the reapportionment cases clearly show? In the background of those cases is the notion that people in places like the outer islands of Hawaii do not need to have a sense of governing themselves. We have talked about the Fourteenth Amendment and the process that began after the Civil War, but it seems that the recession into the shadows of self-government began early with the gradual sapping of the vitality of the constitutional provision—which is very strong—that the United States shall guarantee to every state a republican form of government. It sounds like sending the army into states to depose state governments. It is not clear what it means. But at least beginning with *Luther v. Borden* in 1849, it began to be drained of practical meaning.

MR. BELZ: On the contrary the reconstruction of the southern states was carried out under the guarantee clause, that is, the guarantee of republican government. I do not follow you on the draining of meaning. In fact aren't the reapportionment cases intended to vivify the idea of participation and self-government?

MR. HOWARD: One of the paradoxes of modern constitutional power in the Supreme Court has been the use of the Fourteenth Amendment to rekindle some opportunities for local self-government. I am one of those who bridle at the Supreme Court's ignoring federalism, but I do pick up on Professor Belz's point that beginning with footnote 4 in *Carolene Products* one of the areas in which the Court thought judicial intervention might be most appropriate was giving open access to the political process, aside from protecting racial or other minorities. And I would have thought that as a consequence of a number of the judicially active decisions of the 1960s—such as *Baker* and *Reynolds,* as well as some of the congressional statutes, such as the Voting Rights Act of 1965—although in a formal sense those opinions clearly limited local self-government, they also invigorated state and local government, in that states were no longer free to malapportion or to deny blacks the right to vote.

In fact in this dialectical fashion federal actions expanded the opportunities for some genuine, meaningful self-government and choice at the local level. What the states and localities then do is another matter, and whether they are permitted to exercise such power is another matter. But as of the 1960s federal power actually came into play to give meaning to and to create some opportunities for local choice.

MR. BERNS: On this tension between equality and liberty, Tocqueville said that equality was the spirit of the age. But beyond that, the founders knew well of the possible tension, in fact of the real tension between these two things, equality and liberty. And a passage in *Federalist* No. 10, written by James Madison, the justly most famous of *The Federalist Papers,* makes the point. Here he spoke openly of inequality in a certain sense:

> The diversity in the faculties of men from which the rights of property originated, is not less an insuperable obstacle to uniformity of interests. The protection of these faculties is the first object of government. From the protection of different and unequal faculties of acquiring property the possession of different degrees and kinds of property immediately results: and from the influence of these on the sentiments and views of the respective proprietors ensues a division of the society into different interests and parties.

The first object of government here is said to be the protection of these various unequal faculties, specifically the faculties of acquiring property. In the first place no American statesman today would dare publicly to say that the first object of government is the protection of unequal faculties of acquiring property. Second, if you are a government dedicated to the proposition of securing equal rights, and if you acknowledge that these persons who have equal rights are unequally endowed with intelligence and beauty and pertinacity and all of the other faculties that are exercised privately and publicly—if you acknowledge that they are unequally endowed but they have equal rights—then you acknowledge the difficulty, the tension between equality and liberty.

It seems plain on the face of it, and the founders knew that. They designed the government somehow to protect the unequal faculties of acquiring property, which they had to do to secure equal rights. Our difficulty comes from the fact that we have equal rights but we are unequal in other respects. Can we live with that inequality? That is the situation today because, as Madison acknowledged here, one consequence of this is an unequal distribution of property, different kinds of property, and different amounts of property. And today surely that is one of our political problems. Can we live with the kind of inequality that comes out of securing equal rights?

MR. GOLDWIN: In one sense we can live with it. We do. There is great inequality of wealth and there is great inequality of income and there is great inequality of abilities to get it. Some people get MBAs and others do not finish high school. In that sense we know we can live with it because we do live with it. But you mean something else. That is, can we accept that somehow that is not going to be changed, or can we resist the arguments of people who say that the function of government is to change that fact?

And of course that leads us to the observation that the modern expression of political equality is affirmative action. That and other similar programs are intended somehow to combat what we all know to be the natural fact, an inequality that people have a lot of trouble accepting as compatible with equality of rights.

MR. BERNS: Of course we can live with it. One of the remarkable things in our history is the extent to which we have lived with it. Evidence for this—and I speak as an old member of the Socialist party—is the fact that we have not ever had in this country a viable socialist party or anything resembling it. Tocqueville pointed this out too. He said that one of the remarkable things about the United States was the absence of a proletariat. That was true.

The trouble is that we have professors, and professors are the ones who are opposed to the Constitution of the United States and object to the inequality that comes out of it. This is a political problem, and you have put your finger on one aspect demonstrating it when you talk about affirmative action.

JUDGE WALD: Liberty has grown immensely in its content over the past couple of hundred years, but one aspect—call it the right to be left alone—does easily coexist and is not at odds with equality. Just consider some aspects of liberty that the Supreme Court has recognized—everything from the right not to salute the flag, not to drive with a license plate that says to "live free or die," to send your kids to private school, to have pornography in your living room, not to have coercive therapies to a certain extent, along with bodily integrity, travel, family integrity. We do not seem to have an intolerable tension there between liberty and equality.

But even going back, before affirmative action, liberty involves how you treat other people. We had to go through judicial paroxysms over the older liberty of contract theory in the 1930s to permit state or federal regulation of labor conditions; to overcome the "liberty" of an employer to contract with employees. We were striving, at that point, to define the foundation of the society in which we wanted to live. And that did come into conflict in some situations with an unqualified right of liberty in how you treated other people.

The same thing is hitting us with affirmative action. Society is defining a real problem in living with or accommodating to the long-term effects of slavery. The dilemma we have now is how much to curtail liberty in the way people treat each other by what the society defines as the bottom line it needs to exist as a society.

MR. ALLEN: I would like to attempt a different version of that problem, which Walter Berns and Judge Wald have just described. From a contemporary point of view, perhaps less so from the point of view of the Constitution, the principal question is whether we are to hold our principles hostage to practical difficulties—the same difficulty that Judge Wald noted with respect to slavery in the convention and that is discussed in *Federalist* No. 10.

What Madison was discussing in *Federalist* No. 10 are the kinds of practical difficulties that the Constitution has been designed to deal with. These are not necessarily problems spawned by the Constitution but rather problems solved by the Constitution. In the contemporary world that is not our perspective, and in that sense the criticism is valid. But that may mean we make a mistake in the contemporary world because the problem of inequality as Madison discussed it in *Federalist* No. 10 is a problem of liberty.

The protection of diverse faculties arises from the inability to communalize men in their passions, interests, and opinion. According to Madison to destroy such liberty would be like destroying the air that we breathe because some incidental difficulties or problems are associated with it. Now if that is a problem with liberty, that inequality has nothing to do with the fundamental equality that is a principle in the Constitution. The latter is as an equality of rights, the equality on which the consent of the governed is based.

In contemporary terms this situation has produced a paradox that is perhaps of greatest moment for us as a people. Affirmative action and the civil rights regime in that sense exist as an overlay of our constitutional structures and principles, an exception, an excrescence. Insofar as it is an excrescence, it will always divert our attention from the true principles. Ideally we should be able to live in a society without this massive civil rights edifice and civil rights laws, not without juridical protection of individuals but without the special statutes and agencies and regulations aimed to produce something called equality. This exception, almost by definition, will be at war with the fundamental structures and principles of the society and, persisting as an excrescence, today threatens to overwhelm the Constitution altogether.

MR. BELZ: That makes me think of some of what I have been reading in Title VII cases. I have been trying to think about the relationship between the Constitution and affirmative action. Few statements try to explain that relationship. I have the impression that there is a sense that the Constitution can be suspended for a time while this kind of emergency situation is being dealt with.

We will probably get to more satisfying analyses of the constitutional standing of affirmative action. We have not had them yet. We have had assertions, such as *NAACP* v. *Allen,* in 1974, with a circuit court opinion with a glimmering of an attempt to analyze it.

MR. FAIRBANKS: I want to take up the question of the original Constitution as originally passed, which it seems to me, gives to slavery this peculiar status by which it denies it a legitimate place within the constitutional system but permits it in practice. If one tried to deduce from the original Constitution its attitude toward affirmative action, one would have to use that as a model. I mean that obviously, the attack on hereditary distinctions, which is very strong in the Constitution, and one of the few areas in which the Constitution strays into social issues, shows the incompatibility of affirmative action in principle with the spirit of the Constitution, but that doesn't settle the issue of its permissibility as a sort of prudential matter, I would argue.

EVA BRANN: I would like to ask William Allen, with reference to what Charles Fairbanks just said, if the Constitution is to be suspended for the sake of righting some particular wrong, on an emergency basis, and if it were effective, why shouldn't we do it?

MR. ALLEN: I am tempted to say that I do not think it could be effective. That involves a recurrence to the principles themselves to discuss why that is so, but I will try to accomplish, by way of shorthand, what I think the response is. Professor Fairbanks mentioned a number of constitutional prohibitions such as provisions against titles of nobility and attainders by way of treason, all of which express limitations on the power of government, not goals in any social sense to be achieved by the positive agency of government.

They are expressed in that form because of inherent limitations on the structure of the regime itself. The regime of self-government requires a self-denying principle at its origin with respect to the powers of government. Any time that self-denying principle is rescinded, one returns to the *ancien régime.* Then the question converts to this: Is there any pre-American form of political life that might be consistent with some of the active goals that we seem to wish to seek today? I do not think there are any.

JUDGE WALD: I am not sure there is a consensus that the Constitution has been suspended. We are talking about spirit, and spirit is important. Certainly the contents of the key phrases, such as equal protection of the law or due process, the question of what is constitutionally permissible to ensure equality, have evolved, whether or not one agrees with the way they have evolved.

They are certainly not in clear, bright lines in the Constitution. Many people—and I would probably put myself among them—would argue that the Constitution has not been suspended. I may differ with many of the nuances of the various Supreme Court affirmative action cases, but I do not have an impression that we have suspended the Constitution.

The question of how the Constitution should apply to an attempt to translate equality for some fundamental aspects of our society into real life is something the Constitution can accommodate, even if I do not agree with every one of the Supreme Court cases.

MR. BELZ: It seems that Judge Wald has illustrated why the question of whether there is a spirit of the Constitution has become problematic. She suggests that there is not agreement that the Constitution has been suspended, but it seems like a kind of feeling. And that is the reason why the spirit has become problematic: too many times it is a mere feeling, a subjective feeling that seems to inform judicial opinions about constitutional questions. So the positivists, as Professor Graglia and Chief Justice Burger have said, let us get back to the Constitution, let us get back to the text of the Constitution. And they take it to such an extent that they do not even want to talk about a spirit of the Constitution.

I want to talk about the spirit of the Constitution, but I also want to discuss what kind of evidence supports statements about the spirit of the Constitution. The text of the Constitution would be a good place to begin about evidence that would support statements about the spirit.

MR. GOLDWIN: There is no concept anywhere in the Constitution of group rights. In the provisions in the Constitution, in the amendments addressing problems of discrimination on the basis of race or sex, the words are always "persons" and "citizens." No citizen shall be denied the right to vote for reason of sex or race or age. The notion of a group right in some affirmative sense seems not at all in the spirit of the Constitution but something of a threat to the constitutional principles. And that is the direction that affirmative action is taking.

MR. BERNS: In a sense we all agree as to what the spirit of the Constitution is in this area. This is demonstrated by our consistent habit of talking about it, and specifically the consistent habit of the advocates of affirmative action talking about it. I had never heard

THE SPIRIT OF THE CONSTITUTION

anybody advocating affirmative action who does not exempt himself or herself as one of the intended beneficiaries and who would not be insulted if it were suggested that he or she was advocating affirmative action for selfish reasons.

Second, I have never heard anybody discuss this, or advocate it publicly, who does not also say that this is merely a temporary matter—we will suspend the principle for a time. And then I am always amused by Justice O'Connor's statement in her concurring opinion in *Johnson* v. *Transportation Agency of Santa Clara County, California*, in which she refers to Justice Scalia's dissenting opinion (this is a Title VII case in which the Supreme Court completed its turning of Title VII on its head, much to its embarrassment). Justice O'Connor said, "As Justice Scalia points out with excruciating clarity, we have done something wrong here today." We know what the spirit of the Constitution is very well indeed.

BENJAMIN BARBER: If I were to have titled this session, I would have added another term. I would call it "Liberty, Equality, and Property." We have talked a little about property, but perhaps we need to talk about it even more. It is difficult to derive from the Constitution, even the spirit of the Constitution, an argument that fully supports affirmative action, but that is partly because—as Charles Fairbanks was hinting earlier—in its own time the spirit of the Constitution was slavery. Obviously a document that makes slavery its tenor is not one that will give much sustenance to a doctrine like affirmative action.

Now the Constitution was amended in ways that eliminate slavery but its proclivity to property remained. It had been slavery as property that was protected in decisions like *Dred Scott*. The tension between liberty and equality comes because in fact in the Constitution—in *Federalist* No. 10 as Professor Berns suggests—the primary concern is not so much with liberty as with property and the securing of property.

And when you interpret liberty as property, then there is a clear tension between property and equality. It is the tension between liberty and equality that is resolved in the ancient notion of self-government. But the tension between property and equality that is created with modern government has given rise to a new series of tensions that have plagued our history, led to the Civil War, and continued to create the sorts of difficulties with which we try to wrestle in programs like affirmative action.

MR. ALLEN: It is incorrect to say that the Constitution is proslavery in its spirit; in fact it is antislavery. I am familiar with the arguments that proceed from saying the Constitution permits slavery to assuming therefore that it authorizes slavery, but they are incorrect. There is a distinction between permitting and authorizing.

The language, not only of the Constitutional Convention but of the acts before and after that time, make plain that the weight of the principles and structures of the Constitution are antislavery. The whole assertion of this tension between liberty and property, based on the slavery example, is unfounded. It is also unfounded in *Federalist* No. 10. Perhaps the best way to emphasize this is to restate that I do not limit my earlier statement about the civil rights regime to affirmative action.

I applied it to the civil rights regime, that is to say, that edifice of laws, regulations, and agencies that take as an explicit duty the securing of rights for designated classes of citizens understood as not assimilable to the general rights and privileges of American citizenship. Whatever can be assimilated to the general rights and privileges of American citizenship can be resolved on the grounds of the Constitution. Something over and above that does amount to a de facto suspension of the Constitution and is to that degree also an undermining not only of citizenship but of the founding principles themselves.

MR. BARBER: If one wants to argue that the Constitution was suspended to introduce the principle of affirmative action, then I would say if the spirit of the Constitution is antislavery, the Constitution was suspended for the seventy-five years in which America continued to have slavery despite its Constitution.

MR. FAIRBANKS: It is worth trying to formulate clearly what the Constitution tried to do about slavery and to express that the Constitution permits slavery as a practice within the Constitution, while denying slavery its name, that is, denying it legitimacy under the Constitution. It seems that the spirit of the Constitution intended to do away with slavery. In other words some kind of latent principles are intended to abolish slavery in practice and therefore to knit up that kind of potential contradiction.

MR. BERNS: That is clear enough. The spirit of the Constitution is without question antislavery, but Professor Barber is correct in suggesting that we suspended the Constitution for seventy-five years.

JUDGE WALD: Nothing in the Constitution seems to guarantee or even validate group rights. But we are brought back to the reality that slavery was imposed upon a group. People were not declared to be slaves or not slaves based upon individuals. It was a status that applied to a group of people, to blacks. There were emancipated blacks, but basically it was a racial group practice.

The same thing is true of postslavery discrimination. For the most part it was a discrimination against somebody because of membership in a particular race. One of the unsolved enigmas is, How do you limit remedies for discrimination to an individual? How will that ever accomplish much against a practice that imposes first slavery, then discrimination, based upon the person's membership in a group?

That is one of the dilemmas that we are facing in affirmative action—must there be the one-on-one discrimination. Did you discriminate against Joe? Therefore Joe gets a remedy—but not Jane, who comes along at a later date. You cannot validate affirmative action for her because she did not suffer discrimination. The Supreme Court did not buy that particular argument, but the argument is still out there and is a real problem. The text of the Constitution talks about citizens and persons, but I am not sure that I see the spirit of the Constitution as bringing down a curtain on any form of affirmative action for groups.

Mr. Berns: The question, to use Lincoln here, is, What does the Constitution permit us to do to bind up the nation's wounds?

Jack Rakove: One of the nice things about the bicentennial is the chance it has given us to renew debates in different parts of the country. But this idea that the principles of the Constitution, as adopted in 1787, are antislavery is simply absurd and patently false. If you go through either the debates or the consequences, you are still left with the three-fifths clause, which extends substantial representation to a group of white property owners, white slaveholders, and for all intents and purposes over-represents them. It is not really a general recognition that representation ought to be proportioned to property because other forms of property are not given similar weighting. You are left with the fact that although it was not originally intended as such, the scheme of equal representation in the Senate became a constitutional defense of slavery.

One can point to the constitutional provision that after twenty years Congress could suspend the importation of slaves, although they are not described as slaves as such. But as historical demographers have demonstrated, by and large the continued importation of Africans after the Revolution is not really a significant factor in the maintenance of American slavery because already before the revolution, alone among the slave systems in the Western world, this one had become self-sustaining.

And I have also been struck by the way in which even the republican guarantee clause had a proslavery aspect. Even Madison, whom I regard as no friend of slavery, when he defended the republican guarantee clause to which we alluded earlier, did so explicitly at the convention and then a bit more fuzzily in *The Federalist* on the basis of the authority it would vest in the federal government to intervene within the states, for all intents and purposes, on behalf of the white population—who constitute in some sense a group— against the danger of slave uprisings. Now that seems in some ways perhaps the most graphic—one could even argue in terms of the consequences as they are perceived, as perhaps the most poignant— example of what the republican guarantee clause meant to the framers.

In all these ways, for better, for worse, the abolitionists had it right when they argued that the Constitution was a compact with the devil precisely because of the many protections, political and otherwise, that it extended to slavery.

MR. BERNS: Let me use your precise example about the three-fifths clause. The delegates from the southern states wanted five-fifths. That is to say, they wanted each black person to be counted as one person. Would you conclude from that they were antislavery?

MR. RAKOVE: No, of course not.

MR. BERNS: No. So why do you conclude that the other side, that settled on three fifths, was not antislavery?

MR. RAKOVE: They proposed five-fifths to get three-fifths. It is all part of the argument that is going on. Madison made this explicit, as Judge Wald alluded, in his speeches in late June and early July when he tried to break the deadlock over equal state representation. He said, if you really want to have a scheme of apportionment, and we really look at this country in terms of its factions, we see two societies, and one is slave and one is free. And if you really want to have a scheme of apportionment that takes these sociological facts into mind, then let us have apportionment in one house based on just representation of citizens, free persons, and let us have representation in the other house based on total population, including slaves.

And in some ways, that makes more sense than small state and large state divisions. I agree with Madison's analysis of the categories that are involved here. But the problem is, Madison went on to say, that there is a kind of asymmetry because one house, in theory, will be more important. Presumably the Senate will have additional powers of greater consequence than the House. So therefore you can not really have sectional compromise because of the asymmetry of the positions. But the explicitness with which Madison said in the end that we do not have a multiplicity of factions, we have two, and one is based on slavery and the other is based on freedom—this is what we really have to confront.

MR. GOLDWIN: Then your argument would be that the Constitution is not proslavery, but there were strong sentiments on both sides making both of the arguments that you are making now.

MR. RAKOVE: No, I cannot accept that because it does seem that the political protection, or the influence extended to the South through the three-fifths clause, and then through the later application of the principle of equal state representation, constitutes a positive defense for the slave interests.

MR. GOLDWIN: But the three-fifths clause still left the South in a minority in the House as well as the Senate.

MR. ALLEN: This is an unhistorical discussion to this point. In the first place Madison simply did not break the deadlock, June 29 and 30, by introducing slavery. May 30, a month earlier, he asked the convention not to raise the question of representation and apportionment in order to avoid the problem of slavery. He first explicitly asked the convention not to talk about this because it would break them up. A month later the convention had gotten nowhere. Then, as Judge Wald points out, he brought it in deliberately to try to pass the logjam of small state and large state. In other words he used it in both directions in the convention. A historical account would have to say he was engaging in political discussion, in a deliberative framework. One must not place all the weight on any given moment in that but look at the whole to assess its tendency.

And further, with respect to the three-fifths clause, it does not originate in the convention. It originates in the debates of the Confederation Congress, March–April 1783. The language is very plain: that there it is not the question of race, as a group, but the question of the distinction between the legal status of slavery and the legal status of free men. And indeed in the original version the language is inclusive of every race, sex, and condition. Free men are recognized. When it was rewritten in 1787, it would take nothing more than a good grammar teacher to point out that what was accomplished is economy of language, not retrenchment of principles.

So it seems that for us to argue from these examples a tendency, flies in the face of the manifest language of the founding. We need more than that to say the Constitution was proslavery. Therefore we have taken away that threshold, and having removed the threshold, we have to ask ourselves about the principles of the government, the way it operates. And that is why I have then insisted on the notion of self-government, and its application as the founders understood it, to demonstrate that its tendency is wholly antislavery.

We are making the mistake of Stephen Douglas, who pointed out that slavery is like the family. Now the family is not mentioned in the

Constitution either, is it? Do we say, because it is not mentioned, that the framers are profamily? No. Are they antifamily? No. But clearly our judgment about the family will be based on the practices and habits of the people, just as our judgment about slavery will be based on their practices, habits, expressions of opinion. And in that light, the founding was no less antislavery than it was profamily.

MR. BERNS: On this particular point, Professor Rakove, the dispute between us is this. Professor Allen and I are contending that it is possible to make a pact with the devil and still be antislavery, and we can point to certain clauses of the Constitution. I would say Article I, section 9, with respect to migration and importation, is the best evidence I would introduce. Yes, we are making an accommodation with slavery, we are allowing the importation for a few more years. But eventually Congress will have the power not only to abolish, as it did, the importation from abroad but the power to forbid the migration of slaves, the interstate slave trade. And that would follow from the fact that if the word "person" there refers only to slaves, then quite clearly Congress would have the power to forbid the interstate slave trade.

If that is so, that is language in the Constitution that both acknowledges the pact with the devil, accommodating us, the United States, with the presence of slavery under state laws, and granting the eventual power to abolish the interstate slave trade with the view to abolishing slavery itself. And that is evidence of the antislavery spirit of the Constitution, even as it is evidence of the accommodation. That is the dispute between us.

MR. RAKOVE: To some extent that might be, but it seems that your reading of the significance in those provisions is naïve and overly optimistic. I would be perfectly prepared to concede that the framers were morally troubled, or a majority of them were morally troubled, by the existence of slavery, and their choice of language, as William Allen is suggesting, indicates their embarrassment. The sense of embarrassment in some way testifies to their failure to know what to do about the problem, basically.

MR. BERNS: But why would they be embarrassed? Embarrassed because of failure to do what they thought was right, a failure to accomplish a union that was consistent with the principles of the Constitution, or the spirit of the Constitution, which is what we are arguing?

MR. RAKOVE: No, I would say the principles of liberty, in a more general sense, and perhaps the principles of the Declaration. But if one looks at the Constitution as a political compact, and looks at its consequences, at the question of interstate commerce, and labor importations, these are fragile foundations to rest on, for the reason that these men are after all property holders of men, they are managing plantations, they know their slaves are reproducing, they know that the importation of slaves is not that important to the viability of the slave economy. That is what sets North America apart from the West Indies and from Brazil and other societies. They knew, in other words, that slavery here could perpetuate itself without future importations, and arguably, over time, if you wait long enough, you do not need interstate commerce for slave regimes in places like Texas and Louisiana to sustain themselves, either.

So you could make an interesting counterfactual argument: suppose that interstate commerce of slaves had been suspended as of 1850. Would it have made any difference to the viability of the slave regime? No, because you already have an adequate basis for slave populations to grow and to be fruitful and multiply throughout the South.

MR. BELZ: Your language shifted from intentions to consequences, and when we are talking about the spirit of the Constitution, we are talking about an intent. A kind of grudging and embarrassed concession to slavery does not translate into a kind of a ringing assertion of a proslavery Constitution.

MR. RAKOVE: I am talking about both intentions and consequences, as even factoring in a sense of embarrassment, guilt, lack of knowledge of what to do.

MR. ALLEN: But that is not the perspective of even Madison, who laid out explicitly an argument whereby you can make this pact with the devil, not change a single thing in a slaveholding state, and still come down on the side of liberty. Now you would have to argue that he was wrong in order to make your argument. You cannot deny that he thought about it and expressed himself on it, for he did so.

TERENCE MARSHALL: It might be useful to refer to an observation that is often made with respect to the slavery question and the Constitution. It is quite unlikely that any southern state would have ratified the Constitution on the condition that it abolish slavery. And if the South had not adopted the Constitution, adoption was questionable at the time in quite a few states, even in the North—that would not have freed any slaves. And if we consider the question of a tendency in the Constitution as being capitalist, we should also recall that the South was anticapitalist, and in that case we can recall the consequences of capitalism for diversification of the economy. The founders were looking toward commercial diversification, and they knew that would have effects on slavery. Regarding the number of years in which slavery was prolonged, until the Civil War, it is worth recalling also three historical events that weighed heavily on the South's retention of slavery, namely, not only the cotton gin to which one always refers, but also the fact that those territories added to the Union after the adoption of the Constitution increased the power of the slave states in Congress. The third event of course is the Industrial Revolution in England, which developed the textile industry and therefore made slavery so much more commercially viable.

In that sense then we can say that the expectation of the founders, that the development of a capitalist economy would weaken slavery, was slowed by these subsequent events. But that is not to say that the spirit of the Constitution is proslavery. It is quite the contrary, and we see analogies in other countries. The striking example is South Africa, where the capitalists are those who are most in favor of reform, and the strongest support for discrimination is among agricultural interests in South Africa.

COMMENT: My interpretation is that slaves at the time of the writing of the Constitution were considered chattel. In the intervening years, in the 1860s, slavery was abolished, and at that time slaves achieved equality as free persons. From that point forward slaves became free people and were equal to everybody else in the country. The Constitution covered them, from the 1860s on, as if they were not people who were considered something other than free people before the 1860s.

MR. BERNS: The Thirteenth Amendment obviously abolished slavery. The Fourteenth Amendment in its first sentence had the effect of reversing the decision of the Court in *Dred Scott* v. *Sandford*. It says, "All persons born and naturalized in the United States, and subject to the jurisdiction thereof, are citizens of the United States"— and if I may interpolate one word—"and of the States in which they *happen*"—that's the interpolation—"to reside." What this does is make it absolutely clear that black persons, even if they were former slaves, are part of the people of the United States.

In fact some black persons in the northern states were citizens of the states at the beginning and voted, for example, for delegates to the various state ratifying conventions. We know that from Justice Curtis's dissenting opinion in *Dred Scott*. The Fourteenth Amendment makes it absolutely clear that these people are legally, at least, as the rest of us are, part of the people of the United States. We are citizens. The next question is, How do we bind up the nation's wounds, beyond the legal sense? And that is what we are still discussing here.

MR. GOLDWIN: One other thing should be pointed out. The Constitution does not use the word "slave," but some circumlocutions any time it is obviously referring to slaves and slavery. The slaves are always referred to as persons, never as chattel, and never acknowledged as property. Although they were bought and sold, the Constitution makes no acknowledgment of it, and nothing had to be changed in the way they were referred to because they were always persons.

JUDGE WALD: To complicate the situation further, I will allude to something that usually comes up in debates about affirmative action. Apart from how far you can go to bind the nation's wounds, or to ensure against discrimination based upon color, which I suppose everybody would agree is legitimate to do under the Constitution, is it desirable and permissible under the Constitution for society to decide that it does want representation in the important facets of social life by discrete recognizable groups, because we are a pluralistic society?

The notion in Justice Powell's concurrence in *Bakke* was that a university, as a center of learning, can improve society by having people represented there from different racial, presumably different sex groups simply because that made the quality of life better in an institution of learning. One could make an analogous argument with other facets of society. That is another justification for at least some affirmative action programs.

MR. ALLEN: Slaves did not receive equality from the Constitution, nor for that matter did anyone else, and I appreciate Professor Berns's comment. They received citizenship clearly and distinctly. Equality cannot be conveyed by the Constitution to any human being.

5
Religion

ROBERT GOLDWIN: That religion should be considered part of the spirit of the Constitution is thought to be strange by some in view of the fact that the only direct reference to religion in the original, unamended Constitution is a prohibition of religious tests for holding office under the United States. There are two indirect indications of religion. One, the president has ten days to sign a bill into law, "Sundays excepted," thereby acknowledging Sunday as the Sabbath day. Another indication is the date of the signing, given as "the year of our Lord." As far as I know, those are the only indications of religion in the original Constitution.

We think of the American people in the founding era as devoutly religious people, which makes it all the more striking that religion was so scrupulously excluded from the constitutional text. And yet the force of the presence of religion in the way we are constituted as a people has intruded itself into our constitutional life from the beginning. Many have insisted that there is something almost religious about the reverent way we view the Constitution itself. It has assumed a sort of spiritual aura that one would not have anticipated from the secular character of the constitutional text. Some suggest that this is a direct emanation of the biblical tradition and that we cannot understand the Constitution apart from the covenanting aspect of that tradition. Others argue that reverence for the Constitution is not without political benefits but that in the final analysis the Constitution is designed to avoid or diminish reliance on religion or moral principle as a support for free government.

Let us, then, consider the question, To what extent and in what ways can it be said that religion is the spirit of the Constitution?

JOSEPH CROPSEY: There is, to begin with, a minor point. I am not in the habit of correcting Robert Goldwin on matters of the Constitution, but he mentioned this interesting fact that when the signers of the Constitution refer to the year in which the Constitution is being created, they did speak of it as "the Year of our Lord." But if I remember correctly the year beyond which the importation of slaves would not be allowed, is referred to simply as the year one thousand eight hundred and eight, not anno domini, not "the Year of our Lord." In the text of the Constitution itself, this if not religious, then at least Christian intimation is absent. I take this to be one of those silences of the Constitution that Mr. Goldwin has written about so well and that are themselves articulate.

The question has come up before of the relation between the spirit of the Constitution and the substance of the Constitution, as if there might be some disjunction between them. In the presence of the fact that the Constitution is so silent about religion, or that religion is so present by its absence, it would be well to think a bit about whether that absence in words represents a content of the Constitution that could be distinguished from the spirit of it, if there is a viable distinction between those two. There is something outside the Constitution that may be part of its spirit, and that is the posture with regard to the relation of politics and religion that developed during the Enlightenment. In the ages that constitute the intellectual preparation for the writing of the Constitution, a certain attitude toward religion as a component of social and political existence developed and became what one might call the foundation for the Constitution. The terms of discourse that arise in serious political debate come to that arena from outside, or to put it somewhere differently, the concepts of practice are bestowed by the concepts of theory.

There is a philosophy that lies behind the theory of political practice. That there is a realm presided over by religion and that there is a realm in which the purely secular forces are at work, seems to have been established in philosophic discourse on various grounds between the seventeenth and the eighteenth century.

The philosophic discourse on the relation between religion, or established religion, on the one hand and the political life of a people on the other eventuated, at least in the minds of some, in the constitutional provision against the establishment of any particular sect or denomination of religion. There is a foundation for the constitutional attitude toward religion. The foundation is of course not manifest in the Constitution itself and may have to be invoked to understand even what little is manifest in the Constitution.

I detect three different grounds for separating religion from politics. One of them is a philosophic ground developed in the writings of Hobbes, Locke, Rousseau, Kant, and also Spinoza, in his famous *Theologico Political Treatise*. To some extent the ground developed in the philosophic arena for the separation of religion and politics was the ground of the higher criticism, that is to say the hermeneutics of Scripture. The attempt was made to rationalize Scripture, to show, as

Locke does in a book called *On the Reasonableness of Christianity*, that there is no conflict between the teaching of Scripture, between revelation, on the one hand and reason on the other. This was to approach religion as if it were the same thing as scriptural religion. The attempt to explain religion, and how it is related to politics, was in fact an attempt to understand scriptural religion.

In the second place, on a somewhat lower level, there was the discourse on the relation between politics and religion by writers on politics such as Tom Paine and James Madison. I do not mean to depreciate or disparage their works, but they obviously were not works of exegesis, of scriptural intepretation. They were not attempts to rationalize received religion. They were animated largely by a political motive, much of which could be expressed in the term "anti-clericalism," or fear of organized religion as a threat to the civil rights of individuals who lived in a free society.

On the third level, which I suspect is the level that is much more common in our own time, is an attitude toward the relation between religion and politics that I would call the least respectable and has much in common with rank atheism, or simple indifference to religion. And I would leave it to others to say something about how much of that is involved in recent constitutional developments pertaining to this subject.

EVA BRANN: I would like to add a factor and introduce essentially an anachronistic term. Part of the spirit of the Constitution is that it is precisely with respect to religion that the Constitution is revealed as nontotalitarian. Madison, in his great work on religion, *The Memorial and Remonstrance* (which indeed was not written with respect to the national Constitution but with respect to conditions in Virginia), said that religion was relations to the Creator and that religious matters were too high for political expressions. In other words he made a distinction between a high realm and a practical realm, and it is precisely the characteristic of a totalitarian frame that there is not a high and a low realm but that the whole human being is involved. The Constitution does not involve the highest realm, and that is one of Madison's arguments—religion should not be either furthered or hindered by the political regime because it is above it.

IRVING KRISTOL: First of all, it is a mistake to look at the religious disposition, or lack thereof, of the authors of the Constitution. They were for the most part not particularly interested in religion. I am not aware that any of them ever wrote anything worth reading on religion, especially Jefferson, who wrote nothing worth reading on religion or almost anything else. But they were not theologians. They were eighteenth-century deists who thought it was important to have a vague sense of reverence for a deity, for ordinary people if not for well-educated people. It is a mistake to look to them for the meaning of religion in the Constitution.

The American people decided early, ten or fifteen years after the Constitution was adopted, that this was not just a constitution but a covenant as Robert Goldwin noted, which is why we celebrate the Constitution as we do. There are lots of constitutions in the world. I am not aware that other nations celebrate their constitution the way we celebrate our Constitution, as a quasi-sacred document.

If we look at the history of intepretation of the Constitution, we see that the Constitution has an authority only sacred documents have. The history of constitutional interpretation is comparable to the history of canon law and its interpretation of Scripture, to the history of rabbinical Responsa and its interpretation of scripture and the oral tradition. Islam has a similar history. Any religious tradition of legal interpretation has a strong parallel to our constitutional interpretation, which is taken very seriously and is authoritative. The whole point about our constitutional interpretation is that it is authoritative.

Why should people accept it as authoritative? Not for utilitarian reasons. They accept it as authoritative because they think the Constitution is a document that in some sense exudes authority. This has nothing to do with the people who wrote it, most of whom were fine political thinkers. It was in fact a document that was absorbed into the religious traditions of the United States and given a quasi-religious status, almost from the beginning.

Once upon a time, you could pick a fight in any bar in the United States by criticizing the Constitution. I do not think that is true any longer because of what the courts have done to the Constitution in the past thirty or forty years. But the Constitution is what it is and is as authoritative a document as it is because the American people with their religious inclination made it a covenantal document as well as a mere political or social contract. And the spirit of the Constitution therefore has something religious in it regardless of what it says or does not say about religion.

CLIFFORD WALLACE: I want to make a distinction between different spirits in the Constitution. Many spirits have been floating around here, and some should be distinguished. Some principles that emanate from the Constitution are discernible. We have a tendency to enforce them. There is nothing in the Constitution, for example, about the separation of powers, but from a fair reading of the Constitution, the principle of the separation of powers becomes clear. That principle has been an important part of our constitutional makeup. It is juridical, and we enforce it in a variety of ways.

It can be called a spirit, but it is more than a spirit. It is part of the Constitution because it is a core principle of the Constitution. That differs from consideration of a spirit such as religion. That spirit might be helpful in determining the background of the framers, in order to understand the Constitution better. That is a different kind of spirit. Certainly that kind of spirit is not what courts would use, at least not directly, to interpret the Constitution.

I differ with Irving Kristol in that I think there were fairly religious people among the fifty-five framers. All but three to five, depending on whose count you use, belonged to organized religions, and those three to five were not atheists but deists. Indeed when those who were involved in the discussion could not seem to come together, one of the deists, Benjamin Franklin, after quoting from the Bible, suggested that they have a prayer at the Constitutional Convention. They were essentially a religious group. This should not surprise us at all—at that time five of the thirteen states had a state-established religion.

Aside from the Article VI religious test provision, religion is not in the Constitution because the Constitution's purpose was to protect the people from a national government, from a perceived threat. The Constitution was not meant to be an all-encompassing document that would grant rights; that is a code for how our people should conduct themselves. It was meant to set up a system of government, and to provide some protection from the government.

The Constitution says little, but what it says is important. What it does not say is equally important because it indicates that at least the founders did not perceive any real threat to the people on the basis of religion. That does not that they were irreligious. It speaks only to what they believed to be a threat and what type of a government they wanted to establish. Indeed there are those who believe that our whole government is based upon religious principles. Justice William Douglas, in the *Zorch* case, said that we are a religious people whose institutions presuppose a supreme being. Whether you agree with that or not, coming from Justice Douglas, it is significant.

JACK RAKOVE: Of all five topics for this discussion, this one is the most difficult and puzzling. And as the comments suggest, part of that difficulty is that we can easily carry the discussion in different directions, ranging from perhaps the somewhat technical to the explicitly historical and legal notions of the establishment or free exercise clauses. How do we interpret these? What did the framers mean? What do or should these clauses mean today? We could argue in some ways that religion manifests itself in the notion of interpretation and that our legalism itself is a function of a religious tradition that is historically dependent upon the interpretation and reinterpretation of texts.

No one has yet asked whether the foundation of a republican government must in some sense be a religiosity of the people or at least those virtues and traits that are derived from belief in a supreme being and from living a life informed to some extent by religious values. We could talk about civil religion, which may be a distinct category. It may dovetail the idea of interpretivism as a kind of Protestant or Judeo-Protestant tradition. I would like briefly to reformulate Eva Brann's distinction, with my position representing my interpretation of a Madisonian analysis. Without distinguishing between higher and secular realms, the thrust of what was beginning to take place but had not yet coalesced fully in the founding period was an attempt to distinguish public and private realms and to argue, first and foremost—and this of course is the Madisonian position—that religion ought to be privatized to the maximum degree possible. This is the position that Madison held consistently throughout his life. An attempt to find ways to remove religion from the public agenda and to force it primarily into the realm of private conviction, or private discourse, recognized that religion was important but looked for ways somehow to minimize its impact on public life.

Religion can be tied most directly to the founding principle, in some larger sense, in that the Madisonian effort illustrates more vividly than anything else the attempt to determine what government by enumerated powers or government by delegation means. This was an attempt to remove from the public realm an area of governance that historically had always been regarded as necessarily part of the public realm and still was in the American colonies that become states.

Here is the first and perhaps the most obvious area of human activity to try to separate from the public arena, because to make religion an issue has dangerous implications.

A response to this might be that what is removed from the national realm is left to the realm of the states. We could say, we did not want the national government mucking about in the area of religion, but it remained the province of the states, some of which retained established churches or forms of religious establishment, to do so. That is in some ways a defensible position. But as a historian, I would respond that most of the framers understood that the religious establishments in the states were weak. The principles of religious establishment in the states were also under severe attack during the 1780s.

The point I want to stress is that the analysis is Madisonian. We know Madison in some ways was a libertarian, concerned about protecting rights of property. When he went to the federal convention, he saw this as the greatest way in which factious majorities impinge on the rights of individuals and minorities. But he was also concerned with the rights of religious dissenters. And these are the two principal factors that led Madison toward the conclusions he reached in 1787. Nevertheless there is an important distinction between them because Madison could imagine a system in which religion could be taken out of politics in a way that he recognized as utterly impractical in the realm of rights of property.

As I read the passage in *Federalist* No. 10 where Madison said that the principal task of legislation is the regulation of these conflicting interests, I read him to say this: all acts of economic legislation affect claims of rights; almost any measure, be it preferential economic policies or measures of taxation, will affect someone's interests, which he will immediately convert into claims of rights. As much as one believes in rights of property as a fundamental part of the social compact, legislation will inevitably impinge on them. One looks for the best way to protect rights while going about the task of regulation.

Religion differs in that it can be more purely private, more easily separable from the public sphere, than is the case with the alternative model of property rights. That is the genius of the Madisonian system, which I support on both historical and normative grounds and which I would prefer if I were the philosopher-king. But the key point—to try to tie it into the Constitution—is the notion of delegated power. Here is the first dramatic example of a conscious move to limit the authority of government.

MR. KRISTOL: I do not know exactly what Madison had in mind, but the notion of completely privatizing religion is a Protestant notion, not a Catholic notion, not a Jewish notion, not a Moslem notion. It is a Protestant notion. Madison meant by religious liberty a system where everyone worshipped the way Quakers or some extreme Protestants worship—privately, internally. There would be no such thing as a religious community because a religious community is in the public sphere. A community has certain beliefs, certain principles, so it runs into questions like those we now see in Israel or for that matter in Brooklyn. What do you do on the Sabbath? What is permitted on the Sabbath? What is not permitted on the Sabbath?

I am curious to know when or in what way the Madisonian notion of privatizing religion became institutionalized in constitutional interpretation. This is a peculiar notion of religion, not at all natural, and in my own view, it is impossible. You cannot have such a view of religion if you are interested in religion rather than in extinguishing religion.

MS. BRANN: It is not an altogether fair representation of what

85

Madison thought about the matter. It is true that he thought religion was ultimately a matter of conscience and was—as he himself said—between the person and God. But he also thought that if there were an arena left free for religion, the religions would multiply, there would be many religious communities. In other words he thought that the churches would flourish under this dispensation. The notion of a private religion did not carry with it the notion that there should be no religious communities. He thought that it was precisely the religious communities for which he was making room.

MR. KRISTOL: But a religious community is in the public sphere. A religious community can in no way be purely private. It immediately impinges on the public sphere.

MR. GOLDWIN: And Madison's argument therefore for the importance of a multiplicity of religious sects is in a way an acknowledgement that the religious communities, churches, will be political and will have some political effect. But their multiplicity will in a way diminish the harmful aspects, that is, the ability to affect and abuse the religious rights of others.

MR. WALLACE: If there are many religions, there will be competition among them, and it will be difficult for one to take away rights from another. Our situation is different from Pakistan, for example, where 98 percent of the people are Moslem. Madison apparently thought there would be many religions.

But what Madison and Jefferson said about religion must be put into context with what they did. Although I am a great fan of *The Federalist*, the authors were trying to sell a product. To determine what they believed, I am more interested in the actions of Jefferson and Madison. In the Declaration, for example, Jefferson mentioned God four times. Jefferson was not opposed to the use of God's name in this important document. Indeed, when he was president of the University of Virginia, he invited sects to use the campus for their religious services, as long as all of the sects had equal access. And he thought that the courthouse in Charlottesville should be used by churches. He referred to it as a "common temple." And if there is an intermingling of church and state, it certainly is Jefferson's idea that courthouses should be used on the Sabbath for worship and as courts of law on other days.

Also of significance is that on the very day Madison carried Jefferson's bill to deestablish the church in Virginia he offered on behalf of Jefferson a bill that would punish people for breaking the Sabbath. The idea that Madison and Jefferson did not believe in any entanglement between church and state, or that there was a wall of separation between church and state, seems to fly in the face of what they actually did. It was what they said, of course, that is frequently referred to, even in Supreme Court cases—but seldom what they did.

MR. KRISTOL: If we had held this conference in 1935, religion would not have been on the agenda. Why, after World War II, in the late 1940s, does the Supreme Court suddenly decide it has to start doing something about religion?

MR. GOLDWIN: If this were a conference on the Supreme Court, then religion might not have been on the agenda in the 1930s, but that religion was part of the spirit of the Constitution was not a strange idea in the 1930s.

MR. KRISTOL: Everyone took it for granted.

MR. GOLDWIN: So if we were looking for the spirit of the Constitution, we would be talking about religion as part of it, and, some of the points you made would be worthy of discussion then as they are now. What do we mean, for instance, when we speak of the Constitution as having somewhat of a sacred or covenanting character? What is the meaning of religion, or a covenant, or sacred, if we consider it as something secular and do not mean that it has a divine source?

MR. KRISTOL: Canon law does not have a divine source. It is the law of scholars and priests. Rabbinical Responsa does not have a divine law but comes from the rabbis over the centuries. The same is true with Islam. Not every spiritually authoritative document has to be revealed.

MR. GOLDWIN: No, but the source of it is revelation. That is, that is what the rabbis and the priests were talking about.

MR. KRISTOL: The ultimate source, right.

MR. GOLDWIN: But that is not what is meant when we speak of civil religion or the Constitution as a covenant, an aspect of covenanting. It seems that it is a different meaning of the word "religion" when we speak of civil religion.

MR. CROPSEY: We would be in danger of confusing ourselves if we identified covenanting with religion. A famous political doctrine traces the existence of civil society altogether to a compact or a covenant, the doctrine of the social contract, and it has nothing to do with religion. On the contrary, in the form it has in Hobbes, the social contract is the basis of a theory of the state, which I would not say culminates in, but that has as one of its consequences a thorough subordination of religion.

MR. KRISTOL: But Hobbes is not one of the founders of the American republic. We just celebrated Thanksgiving, right?

MR. CROPSEY: Yes.

MR. KRISTOL: The Mayflower people were some of the founders of the United States, not Thomas Hobbes.

MR. CROPSEY: That is quite true, but if one is going to say that every covenant is religious, one is simply making a mistake.

MR. KRISTOL: You are amalgamating contract and covenant. There is a difference between a covenant and a contract. My grandson was circumcised three months ago. That is a covenant, that is not a contract.

MR. GOLDWIN: That is a covenant with the Lord.

MR. KRISTOL: Right.

MR. GOLDWIN: Right. Do you speak of the Constitution in the same way? That is my question. Your answer is yes?

MR. KRISTOL: One does. Or at least one used to do so.

MR. GOLDWIN: That subject would be the same now as in 1935 and has nothing to do with the Supreme Court and has a lot to do with our search for religion as part of the spirit of the Constitution.

MR. KRISTOL: The Supreme Court has unsanctified the Constitution. That is my argument.

MR. WALLACE: It seems that we were talking about the pre-amendment Constitution and trying to understand it. It is almost impossible to do that now because so much of what has occurred depends upon the First Amendment and the Fourteenth Amendment. Certainly Madison's view was that we did not need a bill of rights. He believed the unamended Constitution ensured protection. He did write the first draft of the Bill of Rights, however, and freedom of religion was included as his third amendment. It later became the First Amendment, and both its establishment and free exercise clauses have been significant. But it was after World War II that the Supreme Court tackled questions concerning the establishment clause, which has been the more difficult clause to interpret.

In the 1947 *Everson* case Justice Black, writing for the Court, held that there was an inclusion of the First Amendment into the Fourteenth Amendment and used the wall of separation language. From then on, the courts have had the challenge of trying to figure out just what that separation means in the context of the establishment clause.

We can do away with the Supreme Court decision for the purpose of our discussion, but it is fair to say that the First Amendment and the Fourteenth Amendment became more significant after World War II. I suggest that the Constitution and the First Amendment were in tandem initially, and they have to be considered together.

MR. RAKOVE: In response to Judge Wallace's earlier point on the Madison-Jefferson issue, a substantial debate more or less between liberals and conservatives follows well-defined lines on the establishment clause. I obviously belong to one of those camps. The examples that Judge Wallace has adduced tend to illustrate the weakness of the conservative position as it relates to where Madison and Jefferson stood.

I like Madison's position for many reasons, but the important issue for us ought not to be simply to offer endless glosses on Madison's theory or Jefferson's high wall of separation. Speaking as a historian, what I find problematic and difficult about the whole enterprise here, is that it requires trying to reconstruct a historical situation—the late eighteenth century—whose results were not sharply determined. It was very much a matter of controversy and debate in the eighteenth century as to what the extent of and limitations on a religious establishment should be, and the limits on the rights of free exercise. I agree with Judge Wallace: questions of establishment are more troubling and more complex than questions of free exercise.

This illustrates the problem that I see increasingly with originalism in general. The need of originalism to get back to some original notion is to try to fix a definite meaning. That is fine if you have evidence for saying that in fact a consensus existed among the founders. But people who study the place of religion in public life and ask what was the religiosity of the American people in the revolutionary era must be struck that there was a debate whose parameters are not so different from what we know today. Madison in some moments, offered positions that any good member of the American Civil Liberties Union would stand up and toast. At the same time, many other framers, and many other politicians and communities and citizens at the state and local level endorsed positions that are very much like positions I attribute to more conservative spokesmen today. Religion today is as much a matter of debate and controversy and concern and active politicking as in the 1770s, 1780s, 1790s.

Try to imagine a graph of religiosity. Bob Goldwin's original statement suggests that the American people in the 1780s were a devout people. But historians of religion debate about what the state of the churches was in the postrevolutionary period. One problem for Jefferson and Madison was that the American people apparently became more religious after the Revolution, especially after the turn of the nineteenth century, than they had been at the time of the Constitution and the First Amendment. That is why there are a lot of problems with Madison's position, and why Madison's position is naïve and optimistic and turned out to be false. Jefferson of course had predicted that at some time we all would become Unitarians—not all of us but the American population in general would be moving in Unitarian directions. But he was wrong about that. And it is often argued that one source of Jefferson's disillusion in his old age was seeing the American people become more devout in the pietistic or enthusiastic evangelical sense than he and others of his learning and background had hoped and expected.

MR. GOLDWIN: But if your historical facts are right, one could argue that the Constitution, when it came into effect, began to promote or encourage and in some way is responsible for an increase in religiosity.

MR. RAKOVE: This is the point that Eva Brann made earlier. Madison in his old age said fairly objectively—and whether he was privately disappointed I do not know—look, religion has flourished, and what better proof is there of the wisdom of nonestablishment than the sects we see multiplying? The early nineteenth century was a period of enormous religious ferment, one of whose manifestations— but not the only one—was the emergence of the Latter Day Saints as a postrevolutionary movement.

MR. CROPSEY: Granting these facts, one would then have to try to give some account of them of course. There is a logical fallacy called *post hoc, ergo propter hoc,* which means that something coming after something is therefore the result of something that came before. Sometimes this is correct and some times it is not. One would be jumping to a conclusion to argue that because of something about the Constitution the people became more religious.

If, however, one were to accept the conjunction of mere facts as having some causal connection, one could do it in this way. If a constitution abstains from making religion a public matter, it encourages religion exactly because the natural tendency of religion is to be private, a matter of conscience, and anything that institutionally acknowledges that, emancipates the religious tendency in human beings.

MR. KRISTOL: Where did you get the notion that the natural tendency of religion is to be private, a matter of conscience? That is not the history of religion. The history of religion is the history of religious communities. It is only Protestantism in its most extreme form that views religion as simply a matter of conscience.

MR. CROPSEY: As a matter of fact, the history of Geneva puts that in doubt. Protestantism in an extreme form was no weigher of private matter. But if we started with some notion that the intention of the Constitution was to make religion a matter of conscience or to restore religion to its private character, it would help us to understand what could be conceived as the spirit of the Constitution.

The more things a constitution designates as private—that is, the more important things it abstains from—the more it departs from an ancient notion of what a constitution is, namely, the encompassing, total regulation and formation of the individual, such as the ruling idea of Plato's *Republic*. The constitution means the education of the people in every important respect. This is the Talmudic notion as well as the Greek notion. Could one say that the more a constitution is a limited instrument, an instrument of limited government, the more it compels the growth of something we have been calling the spirit of the Constitution, that big penumbra of things outside the Constitution, presumably incapable of being described within the limits of a free government?

If a people is to be free, its constitution, according to this understanding, must abstain from many things and therewith allow the possibility or in fact compel the possibility that the country will not be governed simply by its constitution. But all those things that the constitution allows will become at first influential and maybe even in the long-run decisive, and the constitution might then begin to be seen as something that never goes out of existence, never becomes unimportant, but shrinks in relation to other things that become important in determining the life of the people. That is what could be meant by the spirit of the Constitution in a perverse sense because it is exactly not within the Constitution except formally.

Ms. BRANN: That is exactly what I meant by saying that it is a quintessentially nontotalitarian constitution; that is, it does not encompass the totality of life, and it seems that this has a specific, educational effect. Many Americans are fruitfully divided in mind in this way; they are continually obliged to think of themselves in two capacities: as citizens and as private persons insofar as they have fervent private beliefs. And a fervent private belief is by nature expansive. One wants to save not only oneself but other people's souls. A citizen, however, is by nature restrained in his interference with others. That continual balancing of what one thinks and what one is entitled to impose on others, is the discipline we live under, and it makes us peculiarly interesting, both to ourselves and to each other. We rarely find, for example, people uttering an opinion nowadays without saying "I don't want to be judgmental." They are kept in a strenuous opposition between the fact that they do think things and the fact that they do not feel entitled to impose them. By and large that is a spiritual discipline.

MR. WALLACE: The theory that the Constitution established limitations on government, distinguished from affirmatively directing people, is not inconsistent with the history that I have read of the background of the First Amendment. Initially the establishment clause was intended to prevent a national religion from being established. Indeed, when Madison drafted the original First Amendment, it said, "Nor shall any national religion be established."

91

If that history is accurate, it can be argued that the amendment was intended to keep government away from religion in order to allow religion to flourish. That is, government would not discourage religion. How would the framers do that? The amendment would keep a national religion from being established, and in addition would allow free exercise so that all the people could believe the way they wanted to believe. On whom did they put those restrictions? On government. This may suggest the framers intended a more limited role of the courts in this area, so as not to discourage religion.

If what Mr. Cropsey and Ms. Brann say is accepted, then their interpretation of what transpired immediately after the adoption of the Constitution makes sense in view of the political and religious climate of the time.

DICK HOWARD: The distinction between public and private is an essential distinction but open to a certain blatant ambiguity. I pick up on Mr. Kristol's point here. The distinction is not between what is private in the sense of some Protestant points of view or public in the sense of some Orthodox or Catholic or Islamic, or whatever points of view. The distinction is between government and nongovernment. It seems that the thrust of the developments that began in the 1770s and 1780s was to raise the question, What is government's role? It was not the question, What may communities do to define religious practices?

The most distinctive American contribution to thinking about government and religion is summed up in two steps that were taken, and they are two steps, not one. One is from toleration to free exercise of religion. When George Mason was drafting Virginia's 1776 constitution, he used the language of "toleration." Madison said that was not strong enough, and he insisted on the language of "free exercise." That left open a question that Madison had hoped to address, but it turned out not to be propitious for the Virginia convention of May 1776. That is the question of disestablishment, a step taken a decade later in the 1786 Virginia Statute for Religious Freedom.

I mention those two steps in Virginia because they were not simply of parochial or statewide interest. They in fact framed the terms of debate that led finally not just to the Constitution but to the First Amendment. I agree with Judge Wallace that it is hard to separate those two documents. The Constitution anticipates the point in Article VI, providing that no religious test shall ever be required. It is not a question of which test. You can't have any at all. You simply may not inquire into a person's religious views for that person to hold public office "under the United States." The more explicit point is made in the First Amendment, in the curious asymmetry between the speech clause and the religion clauses.

The Constitution says that the Congress may pass no law impairing free speech, but it goes on to set out two prohibitions regarding religion, one touching free exercise, the other touching establishment. There is no clause forbidding government to establish speech. Government does it all the time. We as taxpayers pay for the president, the Congress, and others to establish ideas. And if I do not like it, I, as a taxpayer, cannot complain about it. But establishment is an independent strand of what I would call religious liberty. I resist the notion that somehow free exercise and establishment can be collapsed into a simple unitary principle. They are two strands of a larger argument, and therein lies the distinctive American contribution to the subject.

Why has all this development in case law come about so late? First, the Supreme Court ruled that before the Fourteenth Amendment there simply was no basis for applying the Bill of Rights to the states. Even after 1868, cases were slow in coming about but so were they slow in coming about across the board in civil liberties generally. There was not much jurisprudence under the First Amendment—speech, religion, whatever—until after World War I. If this were a 1935 conference, we would not only not be talking about religion. We would have precious little equality to talk about. The equal protection clause was largely moribund as late as 1935. So it seems that the burst of activism from and after the *Everson* case in 1947 is not unique to religion. Somehow it is not a late gloss, it is simply the fact that courts have begun to move in this area, as in most civil liberties areas, only in the past forty years.

ABNER MIKVA: Professor Howard and Professor Rakove are absolutely right. It has to do with when incorporation became a part of national law. It was not that these battles between government and religion were not going on before that. There was the Scopes trial, the William Jennings Bryan campaigns. The whole issue of slavery was being fought in large part as a religious issue. It was not that the tension was not there. It just was not in the federal courts because the Bill of Rights was not deemed to apply until much later.

MR. GOLDWIN: But that accounts only for the absence of cases at the state level, not the federal level.

MR. MIKVA: That is right. There were state cases. *Scopes* was a state case and a bruising one, and there were others like it. At the risk of being accused of collapsing the difference between the establishment clause and the free exercise clause, I think that the distinction of public and private is useful because the one thing that almost had a consensus among delegates at the Constitutional Convention was to disentangle religion from the state. Their experiences with religion had been all bad: bad from the points of view both of free exercise and of the use of the state to promote religious principles, going all the way back to the battles in England on how to get rid of the church's stranglehold over property, and how to distinguish between secular justice and religious justice. Indeed, the Preamble to the Constitution shows that they were trying to avoid all the troubles previous states had, and to create a state that tried to manage mortal justice under a set of laws that are immortal. Look at what is going on in Israel today: the battle of how they try to live secular lives under some rules and laws that stem from God.

That is a difficult mix to manage. You cannot promote justice until you know what kind of justice you are talking about. If you are talking about mortal justice, you can pass rules. If you are talking about immortal justice, if you are talking about religious justice, those rules cannot be abridged, they cannot be amended. The same is true of property. The same is true of all of the purposes for which the Constitution was supposedly ordained. I would agree with Judge Wallace that the difference between the body of the Constitution and the First Amendment is not that great. A lot of the argument against the Bill of Rights was that it was not needed because the Constitution covered it.

Most delegates agreed that whatever else happened, the Federal government they were creating and ordaining would not allow itself to be entangled with religious purposes or religious arguments or religious rules.

MR. KRISTOL: We are overlooking one little thing. The Constitution assumes, as any founding document would assume, that someone, some institution, or some group is undertaking the moral instruction of the citizenry, that someone has to do that. You could say that the public schools could do it, and they did. But of course the public schools' conception of moral instruction was derived from religion. You could say that the churches could do it, and they tried. You could say that the family could do it, but how does the family know what to teach? The family's idea of moral instruction comes from religion.

What troubles me about the status at the moment of religion and the Constitution is that we are making it more and more difficult for any effective moral instruction to occur at all. We are driving it out of the public schools, creating what Richard Neuhaus calls the "naked public square" with predictable results. We are creating a climate in which parents have difficulty finding a place for their kids to get any moral instruction. This is why parochial schools have emerged again all over the country and why they will continue to grow.

BENJAMIN BARBER: Tocqueville makes the point that liberty and religion depend on each other and yet there is tension between them. Tocqueville's point is that above all a free, liberal, pluralistic society requires the glue of religion to hold it together. Above all liberal society requires religion, yet religion tends to undermine freedom. It is a glue that freezes into a single place the individuals in a society. It has a tendency to universalism, even to dogmatism, the dogmatism of religious truth—with a large T.

No one can deny that religion claims a kind of truth that is sovereign even in a political sense over the rest of the community, and that this claim is in tension with liberty. Locke argues, however, that religion requires liberty and religious tolerance to be exercised by individuals. Liberty is rooted in skepticism, however, a willingness to admit that you may be wrong, a willingness—as Eva Brann said—not to make judgments. That tends to undermine the certainties on which religion depends.

In the American tradition freedom and religion, although they require one another, have been constantly at war, in the way that might have been expected from the Enlightenment. Liberty has led to skepticism, to uncertainty, to the promotion of a relativism that has undermined the place of religion in American life. I do not have an easy resolution. It is true that the two need each other, and it is true they cannot live together. But I do not think that we can bury the paradox or bury the tension by suggesting that the letter of the Constitution is the domain of public liberty and the spirit of the Constitution is the domain of private religion because the two domains constantly bleed over into each other.

MR. GOLDWIN: Related to what you are saying is Locke's starting formulation in his *Letter of Toleration*. There are no two things more different than civil society and a church. The business of a church is the salvation of the soul. The business of civil society is the protection of property. And it is for that reason that you have to have toleration. Locke advises that you must first make the church toothless, that is, strip it of temporal power. Then it can be left as free as can be. The difficulty has always been to strip the church of temporal power and also to allow it free exercise.

JEAN YARBROUGH: To reiterate Professor Barber's point, the country is founded on a commitment to religious and political liberty, but freedom of conscience or religious liberty does not necessarily mean that one has to be in active opposition to all organized religion. If you look at all of the revolutionary state constitutions, you see that the eighteenth century tried many different solutions to establish freedom of religion on the one hand and then on the other hand to encourage the moral principles that they believed were necessary to sustain republican government.

Historians have recently taken note of this. A volume in which Jack Rakove is also represented, *Beyond Confederation*, contains an important essay by Stephen Botein on the religious dimension of the early state constitutions. Botein argues that the demise of these provisions in the nineteenth century cannot be understood simply as a rejection of religion in public life. Rather, interest in the state constitutions waned as the country became more national, and some groups began to look to the national government for the encouragement of religious sentiments.

Nor was disestablishment at the state level prompted simply by liberal motives. In Massachusetts the move toward disestablishment was led by religious conservatives unhappy that the established church had been captured by liberals.

TERENCE MARSHALL: On this question of the spirit of the Constitution, it seems useful to bring together what Joseph Cropsey and Jean Yarbrough said on the distinction between the public and the private as it marks the national Constitution and to link that with the distinction between the national and the federal.

If we look at the distinction between national and Federal with respect to religion, we note that religion was primarily conceived as being reserved to the states and not as a national concern. And when we link religion to the question of the police powers, or to questions of morals, and also to the question of political participation, we can connect that with what might be called the problem of public spirits or the greater democratic spirit that existed in the states as opposed to the national government. In some sense Madison and many of the other founders were seeking to correct some of the defects of that spiritedness. They wanted to correct it in favor of a greater reasonableness. Both are necessary for politics, and in one sense we can understand the distinction of national and federal as equally necessary for understanding the spirit of the Constitution.

We could say that, on one hand, the religious question, by being primarily reserved to the states, is necessary, but, on the other, this points to the problem of religion and therefore to the problem of reasonableness and finally to the problem of constitutionalism as a kind of self-mastery in the form of moderation. Thus the national Constitution moderates this necessary spiritedness.

JAMES CEASER: In listening to the comments, and particularly the debate between Irving Kristol and Joseph Cropsey, it struck me that the difference was really not so much about religion as about the meaning of public and private. There seemed to be agreement that there should be no federal establishment of religion. We could take it to the next step. Probably there might be agreement that today there might be no state establishment of religion, that is, by the particular state. Maybe we even could take this now one step further to the incorporation of this through the Fourteenth Amendment so that there should be no establishment by the laws of a particular community. On that point we are in agreement. But should this idea of no religiosity prevent following customs of a community? Here we move from the active act of establishment by the powers of the state to the customs of communities.

When we equate public acts with customs of the communities that happen to take place in public places and when that becomes our standard of public, then we risk slipping into an irrational antireligiousness, which probably no one here would want to do. It is in this sense, that we might come to a meeting of the minds that would allow some sort of community activities in religion that are far short of establishment. The notion of a wall between church and state, when used to pull down any customs of the communities, at this point becomes a defense really of atheistic tyranny.

MR. BERNS: I want to associate myself with something that Benjamin Barber said, and to pick still another fight with Jack Rakove.

The spirit of the Constitution has had the effect that Mr. Barber suggested it has had; that spirit is, as far as the Constitution is concerned, antireligious.

And it is incorrect to say that Jefferson was mistaken when he predicted, or at least hoped that we would be Unitarians. That prediction or hope has been fulfilled. We just do not call them Unitarians. We call them Judeo-Christians.

MR. GOLDWIN: It seems that we have come to the end of our discourse without resolving the mystery of the role of religion in our constitutional life. I would make the argument, briefly, that this inconclusive ending suits the topic.

In *The Federalist* Madison made the argument that security for religious rights depends on "the multiplicity of sects." The First Amendment is effective in protecting our religious freedoms because it tends to perpetuate and even promote religious diversity.

And if we consider the diversity of opinions displayed among us in this conversation about religion as part of the spirit of the Constitution, we see how foresighted the founders were in deciding to accept multiplicity as a given and to build on it as a foundation for protecting our freedoms.

That we did not achieve unity on this question should not therefore surprise us or cause us unhappiness. In the case of American religion, persisting disagreement seems altogether fitting and proper.

A Note on the Book

This book was edited by Ann Petty of the publications staff
of the American Enterprise Institute.
The text was set in Palatino, a typeface designed by Herman Zapf.
Coghill Book Typesetting, of Richmond, Virginia,
set the type, and Edwards Brothers Incorporated,
of Ann Arbor, Michigan, printed and bound the book,
using permanent, acid-free paper.

The AEI Press is the publisher for the American Enterprise Institute for Public Policy Research, 1150 Seventeenth Street, N.W., Washington, D.C. 20036: *Christopher C. DeMuth,* publisher; *Edward Styles,* director; *Dana Lane,* editor; *Ann Petty,* editor; *Andrea Posner,* editor; *Teresa Fung,* editorial assistant (rights and permissions). Books published by the AEI Press are distributed by arrangement with the University Press of America, 4720 Boston Way, Lanham, Md. 20706.